HOME COOKBOOK
of WILD MEAT
and GAME

HOME COOKBOOK
of WILD MEAT
and GAME

Bradford Angier

Stackpole Books

BRADFORD ANGIER'S HOME COOKBOOK OF
WILD MEAT AND GAME

Copyright © 1975 by
Bradford Angier

Published by
STACKPOLE BOOKS
Cameron and Kelker Streets
Harrisburg, Pa. 17105

Published simultaneously in Scarborough, Ontario,
Canada by Thomas Nelson & Sons, Ltd.

Printed in the U.S.A.

Library of Congress Cataloging in Publication Data

Angier, Bradford.
    Bradford Angier's Home Cookbook of Wild Meat and Game

    1. Cookery (Venison) 2. Cookery (Game) I. Title.
TX751.A52   641.6'91   74-31384
ISBN 0-8117-2134-5

DEDICATION

For Clyde P. Peters
my good and able friend
who is always helping

Other Books by Bradford Angier

LOOKING FOR GOLD: THE MODERN PROSPECTOR'S HANDBOOK
FIELD GUIDE TO EDIBLE WILD PLANTS
THE FREIGHTER TRAVEL MANUAL
INTRODUCTION TO CANOEING
   (with Zack Taylor)
SURVIVAL WITH STYLE
WILDERNESS GEAR YOU CAN MAKE YOURSELF
ONE ACRE AND SECURITY
FEASTING FREE ON WILD EDIBLES
HOW TO LIVE IN THE WOODS ON PENNIES A DAY
THE ART AND SCIENCE OF TAKING TO THE WOODS
   (with C.B. Colby)
A STAR TO THE NORTH
   (with Barbara Corcoran)
HOME MEDICAL HANDBOOK
   (with E. Russel Kodet, M.D.)
MORE FREE-FOR-THE-EATING WILD FOODS
BEING YOUR OWN WILDERNESS DOCTOR
   (with E. Russel Kodet, M.D.)
GOURMET COOKING FOR FREE
THE GHOST OF SPIRIT RIVER
   (with Jeanne Dixon)
SKILLS FOR TAMING THE WILDS
FREE FOR THE EATING
HOME IN YOUR PACK
MISTER RIFLEMAN
   (with Colonel Townsend Whelen)
WE LIKE IT WILD
WILDERNESS COOKERY
ON YOUR OWN IN THE WILDERNESS
   (with Colonel Townsend Whelen)
LIVING OFF THE COUNTRY
HOW TO BUILD YOUR HOME IN THE WOODS
AT HOME IN THE WOODS

The line drawings on pages 14, 22, 72, 79, 132 and 176 were done by Arthur J. Anderson. Sketches on pages 36, 88, 100, 108, 124, 144 and 157 were reproduced by permission from Thomas Bewick's book *1800 Woodcuts by Thomas Bewick and His School*, published (1962) in the U.S.A. by Dover Publications, Inc.

Contents

INTRODUCTION

IN THE YOUNG countries of the United States and Canada, even city inhabitants dwell close to their pioneer background, and the small glowing campfire continues to be part of the North American wilderness heritage, although these days it frequently finds expression in the patio grill and the backyard rotisserie. Seldom are these instincts aroused any more taste-temptingly than with sputtering moose steaks and braces of mallard and woodcock roasted to such a turn that their brown skin seems ready to burst with richness.

This republic came of age eating venison and wearing buckskin. We were weaned as a nation on deer meat, took our first venturesome steps in deerhide moccasins, and saw our initial daylight through buckskin—scraped thin as parchment, greased for transparency, and stretched over log cabin windows in place of glass. Today, the multiplying descendants of these earlier whitetails and muleys can add much to the pleasure of the dining room.

For noteworthy dining, too, there's nothing like the game birds that carry with them the savor of smoky upland afternoons and of sleet-chilled mornings relished in companionable blinds. Then there's the small game, much of it considerable more of a treat than even deer, mose, elk, caribou, antelope, and their ilk.

A case in point is the dam-building beaver, now in civilization often a pest on which there is sometimes a bounty, which provided greater incentive for the exploration and development of this continent than any other animal. Lured by their thick glossy pelts, trappers ventured further and further into wild country, to be followed by our pioneer ancestors seeking new homes. Explorers traveled deeper into the North American wilderness in search of fresh beaver cuttings, and towns strung along their trails. As for moist dark beaver meat, this smells and tastes like Christmas turkey. The fat, white, gelatinous tails, which Vilhjalmur Stefansson included among this continent's five greatest delicacies, go so well with thick pea soup, to mention just one possibility, that an innocent will think he is eating his way across France.

Fresh, plump, rare meat is the single natural food that contains all the vitamins, minerals, and other nutriments essential for mankind's good health. Neither anything else, nor any particular portions, need be eaten. Savory roasts, if that is what you prefer, will furnish you with all the nourishment needed to keep you robust for a month, a year, or a decade.

What's one way to accomplish this in gourmet fashion, to whatever degree you may with, during these days of high prices? By not passing up the small game that is freely available to many of us, often throughout the entire year, and which in numerous cases, as when there is a crow or woodchuck shooter in the family, if not eaten will only be wasted.

Although you likely won't want to go to such extremes, it is at least interesting to note that Vilhjálmur Stefansson, the greatest terrestrial explorer of this century, proved the efficacy of the all-meat diet for human beings by living with his companions exclusively off the country on a number of his extended Arctic expeditions. Stefansson even cured two cases of scurvy on his travels by an exclusive diet of fresh, rare caribou meat and water, exploding a lot more theories.

Then, even as now, an all-meat and water diet was suspect in a number of quarters but Stef, with whom I used to correspond, and a former companion of the North, Karsten Andersen, put themselves on an exclusive all-meat and water diet for one year in New york City, very closely supervised by physicians at Bellevue Hospital, and were found to be in far more perfect health at the end of that period than might have been expected if they had eaten the best, so-called well balanced city fare. Since then Vena and I have lived on all-meat and water diets for months at a time without the slightest of ill effects—quite the contrary—and I am completely sold on it. Several M.D.'s who over the years have helped me check some of my work agree with me on this meat question entirely. However, this does not set forth to be a medical book. Ask your own doctor.

When I was a bachelor in Boston, writing adverising and trade paper copy, by the pressure of economics as well as personal preference my table contained a large proportion of game meat, the product of repeated forays into the northern New England and Maritime wildernesses. Then Vena came along, and we took to the woods for good, seeking what was then one of the wildest and least explored portions of the continent, the headwaters of the Peace River in northern British Columbia where population normally ran one human being for every 12 1/2 square miles.

Here, too by choice as well as necessity, we lived to a large extent off the country on both big and small game which in self defense, now with my wife's and sourdough neighbors' help, I continued to prepare in the most appetizing ways possible. From all these experiences, this book of kitchen-tested recipes has evolved.

chapter one

BIG GAME

THERE IS A self-sufficiency about cooking big game, as though even if the day ever comes when we are dependent upon our own resources for survival, we will still be able to get along handsomely. But one has to go about such cookery capably, for wild meat with certain exceptions lacks fat, which has to be supplied by one's own efforts, and the active existences big game animals lead in the unconfined wild places can make their resulting steaks and roasts dry and stringy if certain provisions are not made to overcome these deficiencies. But it's all most worthwhile. Prepared most advantageously, wild meat brings a woodland freedom and savor to even the deepest city canyon.

Much depends on the animal's being properly dressed and cooled immediately after the successful stalk, but this is in the province of the sportsman. Once it reaches home, the simplest method of caring for big game is to have a locker company or possibly a not too-overworked butcher take over the problems of skinning, aging, cutting, wrapping, labeling, and freezing in packages that can later be conveniently handled in the kitchen. In any event, the animals should be initially hung in a dark, well ventilated, dry place in near-freezing temperatures for at least a week or ten days before being processed, although sometimes this provision is taken care of before one can get it out of the wilderness.

The portions, each ready to use, should be in sizes designed for cooking all at one time. If you are doing the job yourself, wrap them snugly enough to avoid air pockets in moisture-vapor-resistant coverings that will make the packets airtight and thus help to stop drying.

Two layers of waxed paper should be inserted between any individual steaks, chops, or fillets combined in the same package so these can be later easily separated.

Freeze as rapidly as possible at zero or lower temperature. Most frozen game can be cooked either with or without thawing. But additional cooking time must be allowed for meats not first thawed, just how much being dependent on the shape and size of the cut. Lower cooking temperatures are also required, or the meat will be dried on the outside before it can be warmed through to the middle.

So that you can be more certain of what you are doing, you may choose to thaw the meat first for this reason. You must do this anyway if a meat tenderizer is to be effective. Thawing is more effectively accomplished, with a minimum of drying, in the refrigerator in the original wrappings.

Because of its general leanness, most big game keeps especially well, although to relish the finest it has to offer in flavor and texture you should eat it before the next hunting season. However, a plump bear should be used within four months to be at its tastiest. Such tidbits as heart, liver, kidneys, and tongue will keep three months at zero degrees. There are also local laws defining both storage and possession limits of big game.

Unless otherwise apparent, all recipes are geared for four diners.

FRENCH-FRIED VENISON

Don't get started cooking these for a hungry crew when you yourself are famished, or they will keep you so busy you won't have time yourself to eat. In any event, cut strips of venison as long as French-fried potatoes but about twice as thick. Dip in beaten egg and then roll in fine cracker crumbs. Chill 1/2 hour if convenient so that the coating will adhere more closely.

Get your deep fat heated to 370°. Put in the strips of meat, a few at a time, using a basket, sieve, or perforated spoon. Fry until golden brown. Then spread on crumpled paper toweling to drain, salt them, and serve hot. Any that remain will make tasty hors d'ouvres.

Or if you'd rather bake these tidbits, cut them the same as before. Dip in melted butter or margarine, spread in a shallow pan and, turning occasionally, bake in a hot 400° oven until golden brown. Sprinkle with salt and serve. Either way they'll become as famous in your own small circle as the Francis Barraud trademark of the fox terrier fascinated by the phonograph.

VENISON STICKS

Again, cut your venison steak like French fries only about twice as thick. Dip in melted butter or margarine. Lay in a single layer in a shallow, greased pan. Dust with garlic salt, paprika, monosodium glutamate, and parsley flakes. Turning occasionally, bake in a preheated hot 400° oven for 15 minutes or until the sticks are golden brown. Sprinkle with Parmesan cheese and serve hot. These venison sticks are particularly for those unfortunate few who still believe that enjoying deer meat is as unlikely as singing a fugue.

VENISON CHIPS

Here's another one that'll keep you hopping for awhile if you have a hungry bunch to feed. Cut off a long uniform slab of venison whose end is of about sandwich dimensions. Using your sharpest knife, remove slices, from an end of this, that are no more than 1/2 inch thick. Have a loaf of thinly sliced, preferably sourdough bread handy.

Saying there are a quartet of you eating, melt 1/4 stick of butter or margarine in a heavy frypan that's large enough to hold 4 slices in a single layer. Get the frypan sizzling hot.

Using a spatula, lay in the 4 slices and sear 15 seconds on one side, turn, and cook the same amount of time on the other side. Then salt and pepper to taste, tip the contents of the pan onto a hot platter, spread 2 slices of bread for each piece of meat with the juices, anchor a slab of venison between, and fall to. Keep this up as long as appetites and ingredients hold out.

SWEET 'N SOUR VENISON TENDERLOIN

For 4 pounds of venison tenderloin, so delicious that it'll be quickly devoured by a hungry quartet, prepare a sauce by slowly sauteing a thinly sliced medium-size onion and a minced clove of garlic in 1/2 stick of butter or margarine until the onion is translucent only and the grease unbrowned. Then mix in 3 tablespoons lemon juice, 1 tablespoon brown sugar, 1 tablespoon Worcestershire sauce, 2 teaspoons salt, and 8 sliced medium-size mushrooms.

Set the tenderloin in a greased pan and spoon the sauce atop it. Cook uncovered in a preheated hot 400° oven for about 45 minutes or until done to your own personal satisfaction, basting occasionally and testing for doneness. Slice the meat and serve hot with the sauce. This is warming under a tightly clouded sky, below which a breeze chants a slow, polar tune.

VENISON AND BURGUNDY

This is for 4, inch-thick deer steaks, their weights depending on your appetites, cut from a quarter of one of the oldsters of the herd, when you want to satisfy guests who are a little dubious of venison. When the meat has warmed to room temperature, sprinkle it on both sides with proportionately 1 teaspoon salt, 1/4 teaspoon freshly ground black pepper, and 1/8 teaspoon parsley flakes. Then rub liberally with rosemary.

Brown on both sides in 1/2 stick of butter or margarine in a large, heavy frypan. Then add 2 1/2 cups of good, dry, red Burgundy. Bring to a bubble, cover, and allow to simmer over low heat for 1 1/2 hours or until tender, peeking from time to time and adding more wine if the steaks show any sign of becoming too dry.

When the venison is done, fork it onto a hot platter. Quickly mix a can of condensed golden mushroom soup into the juices in the frypan and, stirring, bring to a rolling bubble. Pour over the steaks and serve with hot buttered spaghetti, steaming boiled beets, and cranberry jelly—the more flavorsome wild variety if you can manage, cold and elusively scented as a water lily.

VENISON STEAK

For the utmost in venison steaks not cooked over an open fire, cut about a 3-pound slab of boneless sirloin a hearty 2 inches thick. Wipe the meat with a damp cloth. Then rub with salt, black pepper, and a bit of English mustard.

Preheat your broiler for 10 minutes at high temperature. Then place the steak 5 inches below the heat on a grill that has been well rubbed with suet to prevent sticking. A steak that is not so thick requires less time and should be placed nearer the heat. In any event, sear rapidly on both sides to seal in as much as possible of the natural juices.

Seven minutes on each side is enough for us, but we prefer our venison very rare. Ordinary rare will be more like 10 minutes, medium 15 minutes, and well done 20 minutes. Get liberal slabs of margarine or butter melting over the top, and serve the slices sizzling hot on preheated plates.

TENDERIZING VENISON

Tender venison steaks and roasts are best cooked rare so as to take the fullest possible advantage of the natural savor of these princes of the big game meats. If the segment is not already tender and you want to retain as much of the natural flavor of the cut as possible—that is, if you would prefer not to marinate it—treat it with one of the tenderizers utilizing the proteinase in the juices of the unripe papaya which separates the connective tissues and allows the meat to expand, resulting in reduced shrinkage, better retention of juices, faster cooking, and increased tenderness. For more closely controlled results, buy one of the unseasoned varieties.

Using about 1/2 teaspoon per pound, sprinkle the tenderizer evenly on all surfaces of the wild meat, then at about 1-inch intervals, pierce both sides deeply with a fork so that the grains will penetrate as deeply as possible. With the tougher cuts, cover the meat loosely and return it to the refrigerator for at least 12 hours. Then let stand at room temperature for an hour.

Such use of a tenderizer will cut the necessary cooking time by about 25 percent. Incidentally, mixing a teaspoon of tenderizer with each pound of ground venison before putting the heat to it will give tastier, juicier results.

VENISON ROASTS

A preheated, moderately slow 300° oven, no more than 325°, will give you the best results with venison roasts which, unless your palate vehemently disagrees, should be kept on the rare side. A dozen minutes a pound does it for us, to give you an idea. If you are using a meat thermometer, insert it in the thickest part, not touching any bone. Watch it carefully, for a temperature of 130° will indicate the meat is now rare, 140° medium, and 150° well done.

Don't follow what may have been your grandmother's practice of starting the roast in an excessively hot oven. Searing does more harm than good, driving out more juices than it saves and also toughening the meat.

Setting the fatter side of the meat, if any, uppermost on a rack in the roasting pan with the bony side down if possible, will afford you the energy-saving boon of a certain amount of natural basting. However, with venison you'll still need to baste, ideally with melted butter or margarine rather than with any juices exuding from the meat. A bulb-type baster will make it an easy and taste-tingling task to squirt all exposed portions of the roast every 15 minutes or so.

Too, the culinary value of laying strips of beef fat over the roast, or pinning on thick chunks at strategic points, cannot be overestimated. Naturally, this has the advantage of adding much needed fat to the ordinarily lean venison. It also guards the game against high temperatures and, furthermore, tends to retard the loss of moistness. If you want, it can be removed in time to give the roast any desirable browness.

Another way to improve dry, lean venison is to draw thin strips of salt pork or bacon, cut 1/4 inch thick and chilled

until firm, through the meat by means of a large larding needle. You can even go one step further when the savor of a particular animal is not all that it might be by soaking the fat overnight in a red wine touched up with garlic or some other seasoning of choice, so as to insinuate flavors that otherwise would be largely confined to the exterior. When venison is larded in this fashion, the strips should be introduced so that the meat can be sliced at right angles to the lines of fat.

No matter what, the roast should be taken out of the cooler in time for it to warm to room temperature. Then such a venison roast should be cooked uncovered, without the introduction of any water. It should never be floured. In fact, do not even salt it until either near the end of the cooking period or just before serving, particularly as salt draws moisture from the already dry meat and, at best, does not extend its beneficial influence for more than a very short distance into the flesh.

The interiors of large roasts continue cooking for some 15 minutes after being taken from the heat, this in ratio with the size of the cut and the roasting temperature. When there are parts to be enjoyed cold, therefore, the overall cooking time should be reduced 10 percent.

There are two especially effective ways to vary the taste of the final meal on those special occasions when you'd welcome something a little different. For the first, rub the meat with an abundance of dried rosemary. For the second, insert thin slivers of garlic in slits cut in the roast.

Gravy, anyone? Deglaze the roaster with stock or water, scraping to get the browned residue. Put this in a pan over low heat. Blend a tablespoon of flour with 2 tablespoons of cold water. Slowly add this thin paste to the hot liquid, stirring all the while to avoid lumps. If the results are too thin, a bit more flour and water stirred to a thin paste in the same proportion can be added to give the desirable thickness. Cook long enough to take away the raw taste of the flour.

The use of wide, heavy-duty aluminum foil can on occasion make roasting both easier and cleaner. Tear off a sheet about twice the length of the meat. Turn up the long edges around the rack to make sides. Draw each end corner together with the foil turned inward toward the meat to make a gondola-shaped receptacle, folding the corners upon themselves to make sturdy ends by which the concavity can be lifted. Juices can later be poured from this foil holder to decant the fat and to measure for gravies and sauces.

VENISON PEPPER STEAK

Ordinary black pepper is much too pungent for this delicacy, but you can either buy small bottles of suitable crushed or cracked peppercorns or make your own. For the latter, coarsely grind about 2 tablespoons of peppercorns in a pepper mill or your electric blender. Either that or put them in a pepper bag and break them up with a hammer or rolling pin. Sift out the powdery particles for use elsewhere.

Cut 4 back steaks an inch thick. Rub them with softened butter or margarine. One side at a time, sprinkle each slab liberally with the coarse pepper, then press it into the meat with the side of a knife. Leave at room temperature for an hour.

Get your frypan hot and melt 1/4 stick of butter or margarine in it. Using high heat, sear the steaks for a minute on each side. Then remove to a hot platter and keep warm.

Pour a cup of beef broth prepared from a can of the concentrate, 1/2 cup heavy cream, and 3 ounces of brandy into the pan and stir diligently over the high heat for 3 minutes. Pour this over the steaks and speed to the table, along with steaming white mounds of mashed potatoes with which to sop up every last drop of the sauce. A meal like this is an adventure. You'll ride the wind.

VENISON SWISS STEAK

Here's the place for four 1/2-pound steaks, each cut 1/2-inch thick, from an old animal whose flavor isn't all that it might be. Once you have these, continue the proceedings by mixing 1/3 cup of all-purpose flour, 1 teaspoon garlic salt, 1/8 teaspoon paprika, and 1/8 teaspoon freshly ground black pepper. Rub this into the meat.

Heat 3 tablespoons cooking oil over medium heat in a heavy frypan and brown the steaks, along with 1/4 cup minced onion. Add 1 can of concentrated mushroom soup and 1 can of water and bring to a bubble. Cover and simmer an hour or until a sharp fork can be easily inserted and withdrawn from the meat.

Cook 1/2 pound small-size egg noodles according to the directions on the package. Drain, then toss with a melting 2 tablespoons of butter or margarine. Transfer the noodles to a hot serving platter and arrange the steaks over them. Keep warm.

Add 1/2 pound of sliced fresh mushrooms to the liquid remaining in the frypan and, stirring occasionally, simmer until tender. Stir in a cup of sour cream. Using a perforated spoon or slotted spatula, transfer the mushrooms to the steak and noodles. Sprinkle with chopped parsley. Tip the remaining liquid into a sauce boat. Then, even in the midst of the biggest city, it'll be almost as if you're breathing again the scent of lodgepole pine and blue spruce, of serviceberry and kinnikinnick, and the medicinal cleanliness of the trembling-leaved poplar.

VENISON CUTLETS

Cut 4 1/2-pound venison cutlets 1/2-inch thick and hammer with a cleaver, the back of a heavy knife, or the edge of a plate until they are very thin. Beat 2 large eggs and 5 tablespoons water. Dip the cutlets in this.

Then blend 3 cups of fine bread crumbs and a cup of sifted flour and roll the venison in this mixture. Let dry 3/4 hour. Saute the cutlets in 1/2 stick of butter or margarine over low heat until they are delicately golden. Sprinkle lightly with fresh lemon juice and serve. See if they don't have a rallying power.

GROUND VENISON

Ground venison, when it is most advantageously concocted, has less wild savor than roasts and steaks. The main requirement is to include as much beef—not pork—fat as you like to lighten your regular ground beef which this resembles. No more than 25% is fine with us.

Furthermore, don't get in the habit of using just any part of the animal with the idea that any dried or discolored portions will be covered up by the whole. And remove any wild fat. With these exceptions, venisonburgers can include any deer, elk, moose, or caribou meat that is below par in tenderness and flavor.

Seasonings blend in better if mixed directly with the grind when the meat is to be used in the immediate future, not if it is consigned for the freezer. For each pound of ground venison and beef fat, 1/2 teaspoon of salt and 1/8 teaspoon of preferably freshly ground black pepper satisfies most palates. You may also choose to include 1/4 teaspoon of mustard. Some like the effect of a tablespoon of lemon juice. Shredded cheddar cheese, approximately 1/2 cup to each pound of burger, also goes well.

Venisonburgers are at their finest when they accumulate some of the charred, smoky taste associated with cooking over open charcoal. Next comes an ordinary hardwood fire, thirdly a gas or electric grill. Such steaks are next best pan broiled without the addition of any butter or margarine or, at the most, just enough to prevent any sticking.

If you prefer them rare, you're well away. They toughen rapidly with too much heat. But cook and serve the way you prefer, possibly with salted slices of tomato and crisp wisps of lettuce, and have plenty for seconds and thirds.

DEER TONGUE

If your deer is large, the tongue will be well worth bringing back to camp. Unless you're going to save the head to be mounted, make a longitudinal slit between the bones under the jaw, draw the tongue down through this, and slice it off at the base.

Wash it well. Then put in a pan and cover with boiling

water. Add an onion, a small bulb of garlic, several whole cloves, and a tablespoon of salt. Simmer until fork tender. Allow to lose heat in the original liquid until it is cool enough to skin and bone. Then either reheat in its own juice before serving, thinly sliced, or enjoy it cold. If you've never had this before, that first forkful will be almost as memorable as a first view of Everest from Tiger Hill, near Darjeeling.

VENISON LIVER

Venison liver, if you can get it home in time, can be satisfyingly fast-frozen and then kept at 0° in the freezer for up to 3 months, until you thaw it in the refrigerator just before using. This is all to the good, as it is difficult to detect any difference in taste between venison liver and the most expensive butcher-shop delicacy. Many Indians still construct a rack of green limbs and roast their venison liver beside a small glowing fire while they're dressing out the kill, for consuming on the spot. In most hunting camps, liver is the order of the morning after the sportsman has connected, which is too bad for those back in town.

The only secret is not to overdo the tidbit; the main thing to avoid, in fact, in cooking all wild game with the exception of bear and peccaries. Slice about 3/4 inch thick. Brush with melted butter or margarine. If you're broiling, which is preferable to frying, do so with the meat 2 inches from the heat and for about 2 minutes a side, until brown outside but still red and juicy within. If you're sauteing in a frypan, a minute a side will do the job. There are those, of course, who prefer their liver done more than this, and no one can have any argument with them. Overcooking, however, turns this delicacy into a leathery, tasteless, and far less nutritious meal.

Here's a way to give an added fillip to the traditional breakfast of liver, onions, and bacon. Begin with the bacon in a cold frypan. Saute slowly over moderate heat, forking the strips over and over and, if you like your bacon crisp, pouring off the grease as it accumulates.

As soon as the bacon is done, spread it on crumpled absorbent paper to drain, add your idea of enough diced onions to the frypan, and saute these until golden and tender. Then remove from the pan, season to taste with salt and keep warm along with the bacon while the liver slices are sizzling a minute to a side. End by scattering 1/3 cup of heated brandy over the liver and igniting.

Now fork the liver onto a heated platter. Distribute the bacon and onions evenly over each slice and pour the juices over them. Dust with parsley flakes. Serve hot. Such venison liver will even brighten a morning when your head feels like Cinderella's pumpkin about to produce a coach and four.

SPICE-DRIED VENISON

Here's a durable, delectable way to spice-dry venison that will keep it deliciously for decades. I've still a few chunks that I put up thirty years ago in the Far North from which I still cut the odd slice to delight myself and to astonish friends. If you're camped in one place or are back home with your trophy and have a quantity of fresh lean meat you'd like to preserve with a minimum of bother, cut it into forearm-size strips, following the membranous divisions among the muscles as much as possible. Pull off as much of this parchment as you reasonably can.

Roll each piece in a mixture made proportionately of 3 pounds of table salt, 4 tablespoons of allspice, and 5 tablespoons of black pepper. Rubbing this well into the meat, then shaking off any excess, will give the best results.

You can either drape the strips over a wire or similar support, well away from any animals, or suspend them there after first piercing an end of each and looping in a string or wire. The treated meat must be kept dry. If you have to travel, rehang it upon reaching your destination. About one month is needed for it to shrink and to absorb the seasoning properly, less in dry country and more in damp regions. Sliced thin, it's then really something to chew on raw. Scraped and trimmed some, then soaked overnight if you want to handle it in bite-size chunks, it also goes well in mulligan which should not be further seasoned until just before serving and then only to taste.

MOOSE STEAKS

Spending cumulatively about half of each year in moose country as we do, we've been banqueting mainly on moose steaks during the past three decades, and this necessarily has included moose of all sizes, ages, and conditions. Our favorite moose dish remains steak, and when I read so many recipes in so many different places that call for marinating, and braising, and frying for long lengths of time varying from 20 minutes on up I can't help but be saddened by the fact that, except for occasional use as a change of pace, such formulae waste so much fine meat. With the back steaks in particular, those hefty portions between the backbone and the top of the ribs, I've yet to run into a moose that couldn't be cooked like the tenderest of prime beef.

If you don't want to go to a lot of trouble, just pan broil your moose steaks in a hot bare frypan, first cutting them 1 1/2 to 2 inches thick and letting them warm to room temperature before putting them to the heat. The bottom of the pan can be sprinkled first with a teaspoon of salt to prevent sticking, but not even this is really necessary. Don't use any grease at all. Even any that may sputter from the steaks should be tipped out.

Begin by searing the steaks rapidly for 1 minute on both

sides over high heat. Then cook, at the same pace or with slightly less heat if you want, until done to taste. To give you an idea, a 2-inch moose steak that has been pan broiled a total of 4 minutes on each side is fine with us. Only then, salt and if you wish—I don't—dust with a little pepper. Start a generous yellow chunk of butter or margarine melting atop each slab. Serve at once on hot plates.

MOOSE KIDNEY SAUTE

This is just the thing for a late-fall breakfast when morning-livened mist, which the Hudson's Bay Company men call the ghosts of departed voyageurs, has started ribboning down the slush-hushed northern rivers. Start it as soon as you turn out of your eiderdown by marinating 2 moose kidneys, cut into 1/2-inch slices, for 1/2 hour in 1/4 cup of wine vinegar.

Once the stove is crackling and you're ready with your frypan, saute 2 tablespoons diced onion in an equal amount of butter or margarine until they are soft. Then drain the kidneys, add them to the pan along with 4 medium-size sliced mushrooms, and cook 5 minutes.

Stir in 1/2 cup of beef bouillon, 1/8 teaspoon of thyme, and seasoned salt to taste. Simmer 20 minutes. Serve over chunks of hot bannock, yellow with butter, when in the misty east the sun is coming up like a poppy.

MOOSE POT ROAST

This will give you enough for delectable seconds if you start with a 5 or 6-pound chunk of one of the tougher portions. Place in something like a large stainless steel bowl or an earthenware crock.

Mix with a quart of water: 2 medium-size sliced onions, a stalk of diced celery, 1 tablespoon sugar, 1 teaspoon salt, and 1/2 teaspoon apiece of curry powder, thyme, rosemary, mace, and freshly ground black pepper. Pour over the moose meat and marinate for a day and a night.

Sear the meat with a tablespoon of butter or margarine in a very hot 450° oven for 15 minutes. Then pour the marinade back over it, cover, and bake in a moderate 325° oven for a couple of hours or until tender. Fork the meat onto a hot platter.

Blend 2 tablespoons of soft butter or margarine with 2 tablespoons of flour and stir smoothly into the gravy. Cook until thick. Then strain and pour over the meat, and see if the hum of conversation doesn't soon reach that particular pitch of emphasis and warmth that spells success to the experienced ear.

You can advantageously serve this on occasion with hot French toast made by dipping 8 slices of not-too-soft bread, on both sides, into a well-blended mixture of 2 slightly beaten eggs, a cup of evaporated milk, tablespoon sugar, teaspoon cinnamon, and 1/4 teaspoon salt. Brown on each side on a well-greased griddle or in a heavy frypan. It'll all hone the appetite, like sharpening an ax with the steel singing against the stone.

TENDER MOOSE TROPHY

A trophy moose, especially if he has established himself as the king of the herd, is not the tenderest article in the woods, but this recipe will give you an agreeably thick steak that will make for amiable chewing and tasty flavor. Cut about a 4-pound boneless portion 1 1/2 inches thick from one of the quarters. Rub thoroughly with a mixture of 1/4 cup all-purpose flour, 1 teaspoon seasoned salt, 1/4 teaspoon paprika, and 1/8 teaspoon freshly ground black pepper.

Melt 1/2 stick butter or margarine in a heavy frypan over moderate heat and stir around a cup of sliced onion until the bits are soft. Then brown the meat on both sides.

Mix a double-strength cup of beef bouillon, 1/2 cup of your favorite steak sauce, 2 tablespoons prepared mustard, and 2 tablespoons sugar. Add this to the meat, cover, and simmer over low heat 3 hours or until tender.

Transfer the steak and the onions to a hot platter and surround them with small boiled potatoes and boiled sliced carrots. Skim the fat from the liquid and pour the sauce remaining over the contents of the serving dish. Such moose meat will increase your stature in what, with wild game cooked at its best, is an enviable world.

MOOSE NOSE

One of the great gourmet delights of the North American wilderness is prepared from such an unlikely object as a moose nose. To get at this, cut off the large upper jaw just below the eyes. Simmer in a pot of bubbling water for an hour, cool, and pull out the loosened hairs. Wash clean.

Then return to the scoured pot. Add fresh water, salt and freshly ground black pepper to taste, and 3 quartered onions. Cook just short of boiling until the dark meat falls away from the bones and jowls and white strips ease from the nostrils.

If the sweet tantalizing odors have been too much for you, this all is fine to pick at hot. If you can keep occupied with different tidbits, however, alternate bits of both kinds of meat in a small narrow pan, strain the liquid over them, let the juices and the meat jell together overnight, and savor the whole in cold slices. It's Sybaritic.

PROSPECTOR'S MOOSE STEW

This is popular among gold panners in northern British Columbia and the Yukon where gravel-punching Judge Ray Sandy and his artist wife Frances first served it to me. Start by cutting 3 pounds of moose quarter into bite-sized squares. Brown these, along with 6 cups of sliced onions, with a stick of butter or margarine in the bottom of a heavy Dutch oven.

Add a cup of sliced mushrooms, a can of concentrated beef bouillon, a bottle of beer, 2 sliced cloves of garlic, 2 tablespoons brown sugar, 2 tablespoons chopped parsley, 1/2 teaspoon thyme, and a bay leaf. Cover and simmer for 2 1/2 to 3 hours or until the moose is tender. Then thicken with 2 tablespoons of cornstarch and 2 tablespoons vinegar and place with a ladle in the center of the table.

This is particularly bracing outdoors where a small night wind occasionally wafts the odor of smoke toward you, and when you uncover the Dutch oven to stir, disturbed clusters of sparks fly upward and dance a moment in the blackness.

A moose pot roast can be deliciously cooked this way, too.

MOOSE MULLIGAN

Your moose may vary from a legal calf weighing less than 100 pounds to an 1,800-pound trophy. so cooking methods vary from those adaptable to veal to the barnyard bull that you probably eat as hamburger. Moose meat is similar to beef but darker, and of course it has its own distinctive taste which many outdoorsmen believe to be the choicest of the deer family. Don't pass up a moose just because it happens to be an oldster, as these are frequently plumper than the youngsters.

Mature males are at their fattest and tenderest just before the rutting season which is generally underway with the first full moon of September. They then become progressively poorer unless you're lucky enough to get a young bull that a heftier, more pugnacious fellow is keeping away from the females. At the end of the rut the boss bulls are practically without fat even in their usually rich marrows.

The mature cow, where they are legal, is the choice of the meat hunter once the mating season is well under way. The dry cow in particular remains the preference until roughly early spring. Then the male once more bounces back to the front.

Although some recipes tend to be used more with a particular species, even in the limited sense moose, caribou, elk, and deer are all venison. As a matter of fact, in olden times all game meat was considered venison. There are several recipes, however, that seem best with the heavy, dark flesh of what the Crees call mooswa. One of these is for moose mulligan, especially as it is good with even the toughest, most towering animals. This stew is even better reheated, so you may well choose to double the recipe.

I like this moose mulligan best when the outdoor temperature is an exhilarating 50° or 60° below zero, when trees and land and ice are cannonading with cold, and wood smoke sprays upward in a pillar that seems to support the ceiling of frost that hangs in a shimmery layer over the wilderness. We go out to the cache and saw off a 4-pound boneless portion of a quarter so that it will be thawed, if still chillingly cold to the hands, when the time is ready to start cooking preparations. Then Vena cuts it into about 1-inch cubes.

These she rolls lightly in a cup of flour seasoned with 1 teaspoon salt and 1/8 teaspoon freshly ground black pepper. The good smells start when she sautes a cup of chopped onion with 2 tablespoons of bear lard or bacon drippings, whichever we have, in the bottom of our big, heavy, old, cast iron Dutch oven until they are limp. Then she browns the meat. Since we favor what garlic can do for a stew, we add a minced clove of this herb. We also like, on occasion, 1/4 teaspoon of thyme.

Then she pours on 4 cups of water from the steaming teakettle, clangs on the cover, and moves the pot by the bail to the back of a red-hot stove where everything can simmer cheerfully until the meat is nearly tender. At this time 4 small diced potatoes, 4 small diced carrots, a cup of canned peas, and 2 tablespoons parsley flakes go in. Cook until everything, although still firm, is tender. Correct the seasoning with salt and pepper if necessary.

For gravy, strain out the meat and vegetables. You can then thicken the liquid with 2 tablespoons cornstarch for every cup of broth, mixing this first with a little cold water and then stirring it in smoothly. Simmer, still stirring, for 2 minutes. Then mix everything together again and bring back to a simmer.

If you are going to include dumplings, before returning the solids you will have added enough boiling water to give you your original 4 cups of fluid. A good way to go about these tasty and rapidly cooked tidbits is by sifting together 2 cups of flour, 1 tablespoon double-action baking powder, and 1 teaspoon salt. Work in a tablespoon of butter, margarine, or bear lard. When all is ready to go, pour 3/4 cup milk into a cavity dented in the center of the flour mixture. Mix everything together very lightly and quickly, using a folding motion.

Have the mulligan bubbling gently, not rapidly as this would break up the dumplings. Immediately place a single layer of rounded tablespoons of the batter in the broth atop the solids. Cover at once and allow everything to steam for 15 to 20 minutes, whereupon the dumplings should be as light and feathery as the flakes of frost that are scintillating in the outside air. To keep them this way, serve them to one side of the gravy. By this time you'll be so hungry that you won't be able to wait a moment longer.

HEAVENLY MOOSE STEW

This is superb enough to make an innocent think he is eating his way across Europe where, incidentally, what we

in North America know as moose are called elk. You'll need
2 pounds of a fresh red quarter, whittled into bite-sized
cubes.

Saute these atop the stove in the bottom of a Dutch oven,
along with 1/4 stick of butter or margarine, or preferably 4
tablespoons of bear lard if you have it, until thoroughly
browned. Add 3 cups of water in which 6 beef bouillon
cubes or the equivalent in powder or paste have been
dissolved, a cup of a good dry red wine, a large diced onion,
3 sliced carrots, 1 teaspoon salt, 1/2 teaspoon paprika, 1/4
teaspoon parsley flakes, 1/8 teaspoon freshly ground black
pepper, and a bay leaf. Cover and keep at a bubble for 1 3/4
hours or until the *mooswa*, as the Crees call it, proves to be
fork tender.

Keep uncovered long enough to drop in a dozen whole
white onions and 8 small new potatoes, both of course

peeled. Then clang the lid back on, bring again to a simmer, and cook ¼ hour longer or until the potatoes and carrots are barely tender.

Mix 2 tablespoons apiece of sifted flour and butter or margarine into a paste, remove the lid, and stir smoothly into the mulligan, continuing to stir until the bubbling concoction thickens.

I like this best with hot buttered slices of crusty sourdough bread. Incidentally, there is now a Bradford Angier Sourdough Mix on the market, retailing at a dollar, which when used according to the enclosed directions will give you such substantial and delicious loaves for the rest of you life. If your store does not yet stock this, write Chuck Wagon Foods, Micro Drive, Woburn, Massachusetts 01801.

MOOSE MEAT BALLS

Cut into pieces and run twice through the fine blade of your grinder 2 pounds of the lean, toughish meat cut from that part of a forequarter closest to the foot, along with 1/2 pound of salt pork and 8 slices of sourdough bread. Add 2 lightly beaten eggs, 2 teaspoons salt, 1 teaspoon allspice, 1/2 teaspoon nutmeg, 1/2 teaspoon monosodium glutamate, and 1/4 teaspoon freshly ground black pepper.

Mix thoroughly. Then mold lightly with your fingers into about 1-inch balls, taking care to make these uniform so that they will cook evenly. Roll around in a frypan with 2 tablespoons of butter or margarine until they are uniformly brown.

Now beat 2 eggs until fluffy. Add 4 tablespoons finely minced dill, 2 1/2 tablespoons lemon juice, 2 teaspoons grated onion, 2 teaspoons salt, and 1/4 teaspoon freshly ground black pepper. Finally, stir in 3 cups sour cream. Heat, continuing to stir.

Then add the meat balls and cover. Cook over very low heat 1 1/2 hours, adding more sour cream if this should prove necessary to keep the meat from sticking. Try this with hot rice, noodles, or an 8-ounce package of sparingly cooked spaghetti. Such a meal will be one of the triumphs of planning and sheer laborious effort that pass as spontaneousness.

ROAST BEAR

With all the stories that are going around you'll likely be unable to credit the truth until you smell properly prepared bear meat cooking, then sampled it yourself. But with the single exception of mountain sheep a young bear is the most toothsome article you're likely to bag any year. Incidentally, you'll only be disguising a lot of delicious flavor if you marinate the meat as most recipes suggest.

One fact that turns off a lot of hunters is that the culinary efforts they sit down to stop and end with steaks. The meat is too stringy for this, an effect that is heightened by the fact that, like pork, bear meat must be cooked until well done if you are to avoid the danger of trichinosis; neither characteristic being conducive to good steaks. But roast, braise, or stew your bear cuts, and that's an entirely different matter.

Except in the springtime when the bear is ordinarily lean from the long winter's sleep, trim off all but about 1/4 inch of the fat, saving this for rendering. If the bear is lean, however, bard generously with beef fat. Too, then baste about every 10 minutes after the first hour.

Set the meat on a rack in an open pan, the bone if any toward the bottom. Do not season, flour, or sear. A moderate oven, only about 325°, will serve best. Bear varies so much in texture that the only rule that can be given, outside of the fact that it must be well done, is to roast it until a large sharp fork can be easily inserted and withdrawn. Then be ready for one of the gourmet delights of the North American wilderness.

Meanwhile be simmering together in salted water until they are soft 4 medium-sized diced potatoes, a large sliced onion, a sliced stalk of celery, and a small sliced carrot. Drain and then either run through the blender or press through a collander. Season to taste with salt, freshly ground black pepper, and cayenne. Just before serving, stir in a cup of sour cream and sprinkle with chopped parsley or chives. With your share of the roast atop each portion, this repast will be as memorable as that first scent of a rain-shining eucalyptus grove.

BEAR CASSEROLE

This one is too fine for all but the very good. The bear chops you'll be needing should be cut somewhat thinly, so for a robust meal for four you'll want 8 of them. If it's well along in the season, slice off the fat and melt some of it in your skillet to start things off. If the bruin is just awake from its winter's sleep, use ¼ stick of butter or margarine in which to brown the meat appetizingly on both sides.

While it's filling the kitchen with its beeflike fragrance, peel and thinly slice 2 large potatoes. Also slice 4 medium-size onions and 1/2 pound mushrooms.

Spread a layer of potatoes across the bottom of a well-greased casserole. Follow with layers of mushrooms and onions, keeping up the sequence until all your vegetables are inside. Pour a can of condensed cream of mushroom soup over everything. Top with sprinkles of 1/8 teaspoon apiece of oregano, parsley flakes, and paprika. Salt and pepper to taste. Roof with the bear chops, cover, and bake in a moderate 350° oven for an hour.

Served with a freshly prepared green salad, crisp as a ginger cookie from a heavy tight jar; this is as haunting as the Trevi Fountain with its clatter of hillside brooks, like the music of Respighi.

BRITISH COLUMBIA BOILED BEAR DINNER

This dinner is so good that most years we corn some slabs of bear meat so that we can enjoy it several times during the long white winter. If you'll start out with a 4-pound slab, brisket preferred, you will have enough to warm up for seconds whose taste will be even savorier. In any event, first wash this corned meat well in cold water to remove the exterior brine. Then put in a Dutch oven or large kettle, cover with cold water, and bring slowly to a boil. Cook 5 minutes, spoon off the scum, lower the heat, cover, and simmer 4 hours or until tender. Then fork out the bear meat and keep in a warm place.

Skim the excess fat from the broth. Add 8 whole small white onions, but unless they are also small, slice the 8-apiece potatoes, carrots, and parsnips or turnips, whichever you like better. Simmer, uncovered, 15 minutes. Then put in a cabbage, cored and divided into eighths, and cook some 15 minutes more or until all the vegetables are tender. Finally, return the meat long enough to rewarm it.

Serve the bear on a large hot platter with the vegetables and gravy. The recipe is like grass in the sun. Each time you enjoy it anew it's like another refreshing ripple of wind.

Incidentally, horseradish helps bring out the taste. If the mouth-tingling white roots grow where you live, you're in luck, for there is little comparison between the freshly grated condiment you can prepare yourself, using the wild roots and lemon juice instead of the commonly employed wine vinegar, and that from a store. The nose-stinging roots, so good when used in moderation with less piquant foods, happen to be edible the year around.

BEAR PAWS

The small ones are best, 1 to a diner. Skin them carefully, which you'll want to do anyway if you're keeping the hide for a rug. Brown well in a frypan with 3 tablespoons of butter or margarine. Then move to a casserole. Season with 1 teaspoon salt, 1 teaspoon thyme, 1 teaspoon cinnamon, and 1/8 teaspoon freshly ground black pepper.

Cook 2 minced, medium-size onions in the fat until the bits are soft and just beginning to tan. Then scrape the contents of the frypan over the paws. Add 1 cup of beef bouillon. Lay 8 slices of bacon over the top, cover, and cook in a moderate 325° oven for 3 hours or until tender. This is good with buttered, steaming hot spaghetti, especially when gusts of hail, loud as chilled shot, are hammering the dining room windows.

BAKED BEAR CHOPS

Trim all but about 1/4 inch of any fat from the chops, which for this recipe should be about 1 1/2 inches thick. Set in a deep baking pan. Strew with salt and freshly ground black pepper to taste.

Spread a teaspoon of brown sugar atop each chop and place a slice of lemon atop each. Mix a cup of tomato catsup and a cup of water, more of both if necessary, and barely cover the chops with the fluid. Bake in a moderate 325° oven 1 1/2 hours or until well done and tender.

STUFFED BEAR CHOPS

Trim most of the fat if any from 4 large chops. Season to taste, proportionately with 1 teaspoon salt, 1/2 teaspoon paprika, and 1/8 teaspoon freshly ground black pepper. Pour in enough water to reach within 1/4 inch of the top of the meat. Cover tightly and simmer over low heat for 1/2 hour.

Then flatten 2 tablespoons of raw rice over each chop. Scatter a minced clove of garlic across the quartet. Atop each lay a large slice of tomato, a broad thin slice of onion, and a slice of green pepper. Pour in enough bubbling water to reach the top of the meat. Cover and bake in a moderate 325° oven 1/2 hour or until the chops are well done. After that first taste, it'll all seem as fabulous as a princess on a milk white steed.

BEAR CHOPS AND SOUR CREAM

As always with bear, unless it's during the lean months of spring, trim most of the fat from the 4 chops which should be about 2 inches thick. Rub with proportionately 1 teaspoon garlic salt, 1/2 teaspoon parsley flakes, and 1/8 teaspoon freshly ground black pepper.

Starting with a cold frypan, tan 4 strips of diced bacon and brown the chops in the fat. Then set the quartet in the bottom of a baking pan.

Keeping the frypan hot but not smoking, add 1/2 cup water, 1/2 cup sour cream, 2 tablespoons cider vinegar, 1 tablespoon sugar, 1 tablespoon soy sauce, and a bay leaf. As soon as this comes to a bubble, pour over the chops. Cover them and bake in a moderate 325° oven for 1 3/4 hours. They'll then have an almost Oriental effusiveness.

BEAR KIDNEYS

"If I could just eat once more, I'd sure pick bear kidneys," mine-owner King Gething told me up on the headwaters of the Peace River in northern British Columbia. "I'd want them simmered awhile with butter, salt, cloves, celery if I had any, and a mite of onion. Matter of fact, let's get 'em on the fire before somebody else shows up."

Cut or divide the kidneys into segments about the size of chicken hearts. All you have to do with bear kidneys to achieve this is to strip away the connective membrane. Let the kidneys and other ingredients simmer over low heat until tender. Best way to establish proportions is by taste.

These kidneys are especially tasty atop steaming mountains of mashed potato or hot crusty bannock, streaming with butter or margarine.

BEAR CRACKLINGS

The best shortening ever for pie pastries is that which can be rendered from black bear fat. Cut this into cubes the size of small walnuts, distribute in oven pans, and bake in moderate heat until all the liquid comes out. Strain this into jars and store where it is cold. Use just like the pure white lard it resembles but surpasses.

Grizzly fat renders into a most easily measured oil. The resulting cracklings of both are tasty and enjoyably crisp to nibble at although you'll probably have too many, in which case give your dog a healthy treat. The aroma that permeates the kitchen after such a rendering session is delectably beefy.

Here's the opportunity, too, to enjoy some of the crackling corn cakes that our pioneer ancestors relished. Sift together 2 cups cornmeal, stone-ground if you want to be traditional, 1 1/2 teaspoons double-action baking powder, 1 teaspoon salt, and 1/2 teaspoon baking soda.

Beat together 2 eggs, 1 cup buttermilk, and 2 tablespoons of melted bear renderings. Stir this into the cornmeal mixture, along with 3/4 cup of finely crushed bear cracklings.

You should have a stiff batter. If it seems to be too moist, add cornmeal. If too stiff to pour from a spoon, add a bit more buttermilk.

Have another 2 tablespoons of bear lard heating in a frypan. Drop the mixture from a tablespoon to spread into about a dozen individual cakes. Brown slowly, turning. These will really turn back the years, and delightfully.

BRAISED BEAR

This recipe, which has been shared with us by our friends Lt. Colonel Frederick W. Brown and Betty Brown, is especially tasty with any bear. It becomes even better, somehow, warmed up, so start with 4 pounds of lean bear meat cut into bite-size portions. Roll in a seasoned flour mixture made proportionately with 1 cup sifted flour, 1 teaspoon garlic salt, 1 teaspoon paprika, 1/4 teaspoon parsley flakes, and 1/8 teaspoon freshly ground black pepper.

Begin bronzing the meat in 1/2 cup olive oil or other good vegetable oil. When this has progressed far enough for the color to begin to change, add 8 large sliced carrots, 1 large thinly sliced onion, and 2 thinly sliced green peppers, and brown these as well.

Then add 2 large cans of tomatoes and simmer the combination 2 hours or until the meat is tender. Serve over steaming rice. If you enjoy this as much as we think you will, then let's hear it for the Colonel and his lady.

GRIZZLY STEW

You'll want at least a stew made from your trophy, while if your *Ursus horribilis* is no more than about three years old and plump, it will give you some surprisingly delicious roasts. Trim off most of the fat if it's fall and the bear has been fattening up for the winter on berries. Incidentally, grizzly do not hibernate. Neither do black bear, for that matter, both of them settling for easily disturbed snoozes. But the grizzly is out and roaming more than the blacky during the cold months.

For stew cut the meat into about 1-inch cubes, keeping the size and shape of these reasonably uniform so that the cooking can progress more evenly. The majority of the warm months, unless the country is particularly poor, you can brown the grizzly meat in its own fat in the bottom of the pan. The remainder of the time, start with a small amount of butter or margarine, with former bear renderings, or with beef fat. The majority of recipes call for pork fat in connection with lean bear, but in taste bear meat is far, far closer to beef. In fact, when a young bear is cooking unadorned and unmarinated you can't tell the difference from prime steer meat as far as smell is concerned or even later, usually, when you're eating it.

For about a 4-pound chunk of grizzly, which will make enough stew for four hungry hunters, brown 2 medium-size sliced onions in the bottom of the stew pan along with the cubed meat. Then pour in enough boiling water to immerse everything. Cover snugly and simmer, not boil, until a bit of meat you spear out proves to be barely tender. Then add 4 quartered potatoes, 4 sliced carrots, and a couple of sliced parsnips, all medium-size, along with a cup of diced celery and a dozen small white onions. Cook only until the vegetables are tender, salt and pepper to taste, and serve with plenty of buttered hot bannock or dumplings.

For some elusively flavored dumplings worthy of such a dish, thoroughly mix 2 cups of sifted all-purpose flour, a tablespoon double-action baking powder, and 1/4 teaspoon apiece of parsley flakes, marjoram, celery seed, sage, paprika, thyme, and sweet basil. Only when everything is ready to go, stir in enough cold water, about 3/4 cup, to make a thin batter with enough body to lift out by the rounded spoonful. Drop by the tablespoon atop the bubbling stew and cook, uncovered for 10 minutes. Then clamp on the lid and cook another 10 minutes. Served at once, these will be feather-light, and when you start to eat the hours will stand still.

By the way, it's sound operating procedure to make more of this grizzly stew than you all can consume at the first sitting, for even its basic savoriness gets better each time it's reheated.

BROWN BEAR RAGOUT

Cut 4 pounds of lean meat into 1-inch cubes. In a large heavy frypan or Dutch oven, saute a large chopped onion and a clove of garlic in a stick of butter or margarine until the onion starts to tan. Then take out the garlic.

Add the cubes, 2 teaspoons paprika, 1 teaspoon salt, 1/2 teaspoon parsley flakes, and 1/8 teaspoon freshly ground black pepper. Stir the bits of meat until they are well browned. Then add a large can of tomatoes, cover, and let bubble for an hour. If you have any domestic or wild celery, and Alaska abounds with this latter in the form of seacoast *angelica*, stir in 2 diced cups of this. Cook for about another hour or until the meat is tender.

At the end, add a small can of sliced mushrooms. Then blend 1/4 cup of flour with a small amount of water and stir slowly and smoothly into the ragout until the liquid thickens and the raw taste is gone from the flour.

Because of the tomatoes, this ragout is particularly good with cornmeal mush. A double boiler, if you have or can contrive one, makes this latter a cinch. Bring 3 cups of water and 1 teaspoon salt to a boil in the upper pot, directly atop the heat. Have a cup of cornmeal mixed with a cup of cold water. Now add this bit by bit to the boiling water, stirring. Reduce the heat and cook, still stirring, until the mixture comes to a bubble.

Meanwhile, have water boiling in the lower pan. Cover the cornmeal and place that upper pot atop the pan with the boiling water. Stirring every now and then, cook some 3/4 hours or until smooth and thick. Top with cheese and let this melt. Sprinkle with paprika. Then serve everything together. It'll work a miracle on your mood.

POLAR BEAR CARBONADOS

Almost every part of North American animals is good to eat — the Indians even roast and relish the deer family's antlers while these are still in velvet. An exception is the liver of the polar bear, and of the ringed and bearded seal, which becomes so rich in Vitamin A at certain times of the year that it is poisonous even to dogs. But if you're lucky enough to bag a polar bear, you'll want at least to sample the meat, and the following recipe is good enough for a big-game banquet.

For four of you, though, cut at least a 4-pound boneless chuck into 1-inch cubes. Dredge in proportionately 1 cup flour, 1 teaspoon salt, and 1/8 teaspoon freshly ground black pepper. Heat 1/3 cup butter or margarine, bear renderings, or cooking oil in a Dutch oven and saute 8 medium-size sliced onions until they are soft and just beginning to tan. Then remove the onions. Fork around the meat in the grease until it is thoroughly browned.

Put back the onions, along with a large minced clove of garlic, 2 tablespoons of parsley flakes, 1/2 teaspoon thyme, and 1/4 teaspoon paprika. Immerse everything in 2 12-ounce portions of bear. Cover and bake in a slow 300° oven for 3 hours or until tender.

This is good with hashed brown potatoes, started by mixing 2 cups of finely chopped boiled potatoes with a tablespoon of flour and 1/2 teaspoon salt. Then stir in 1/3 cup evaporated milk. Melt 3 tablespoons butter or margarine in a heavy frypan, spread and pat the potatoes evenly across the base, and cook slowly until brown in the bottom. Put a large plate over the top of the frypan, turn both so that the potatoes come out whole on the plate, add another 3 tablespoons of butter or margarine to the frypan, and slide the potatoes back in to bronze on the other side. Sprinkle with parsley flakes and paprika and serve hot with the seething bear meat. It'll be an exquisite moment.

CARIBOU BRISKET

Caribou, North America's most abundant game animal, is

generally tender and tasty because of its leisurely diet of lichen, grass, stunted shrubs, twigs, and flowering wild edibles in a radiant northland where, above the Arctic Circle, no vegetation is poisonous to human beings with the exception of one breed of mushrooms. But caribou do tend to be lean much of the year and are then the better for larding.

However, a bull when at its sleekest and tastiest just before the fall rut is something else again, and at this time the fat brisket especially is memorable. For 4 thick slices of this, saute a cup of chopped onion and another of chopped celery in 2 tablespoons of butter or margarine. Point this up with a teaspoon of seasoned salt. Add the contents of a small can of mushrooms, mix everything with a cup of dry bread crumbs, and spoon over the meat.

Lay the slabs in a flat pan and slide into a hot 425° oven for browning 10 minutes on one side and the same time on the other. Lower the heat to a moderate 325° for the next hour, if you can wait that long, and then fall to. This is something special when the sweet, musty, fall fragrance of wild jam making also fills the kitchen.

CARIBOU STEAK IN CASSEROLE

Cut 4 pounds of boneless steak 1-inch thick from the tougher portion of a caribou quarter and separate into 1-pound servings.

Place in a glass, crockery, earthenware, or stainless steel container. Add a cup of dry Burgundy, 3 tablespoons vegetable oil, a minced clove of garlic, and 1/2 teaspoon dried rosemary. Marinate 1 1/2 hours, then, saving the liquid, remove the steaks and wipe each dry with paper toweling.

Starting with a cold frypan, cook 8 slices of bacon over moderate heat until they are golden brown. Then remove the bacon, break it up, and put to one side. Brown the meat on both sides in the remaining grease. Then lay the steaks in a large casserole. Add the bits of bacon and a 1½-pound package of frozen stew vegetables.

Pour off all but about 2 tablespoons of the bacon fat and juices from the frypan. Sprinkle what remains with flour and mix well. Slowly and smoothly stir in the marinade, along with a double-strength cup of beef bouillon or the equivalent. Bring to a simmer.

Turn this over the caribou and vegetables in the casserole and warm everything to a bubble. Cover and bake in a moderate 350° oven for about 2 hours or until the steaks are tender. They'll then put you in a mood for celebrating.

CARIBOU TONGUE

Caribou tongue, like that from the moose, is a delicacy. Cut out the same way, making a slit under the lower jaw, drawing the tongue down through this, and severing it at the root. Scrub it well but, as with all game meat, do not soak. Instead, cover with boiling water. Add a sliced onion, a quartered clove of garlic, 1 tablespoon salt, 1/4 teaspoon freshly ground black pepper, 6 whole cloves, and a bay leaf.

Simmer about 1 hour per pound or until a sharp fork can be easily inserted and withdrawn. Then fork out the tongue, immerse in cold water, slit the skin and peel it off, and cut out the bones and gristle at the thick end. The tongue can then be reheated in its own juice before serving, thinly sliced, or it can be relished cold.

Or for something special, saute a pound of fresh sliced mushrooms in 3 tablespoons butter or margarine. Add 2 cans of concentrated mushroom soup and 1/2 can water. Bring to a simmer. Season with 1/2 teaspoon nutmeg, 1/4 teaspoon cinnamon, and 1/8 teaspoon cloves. Add a jigger of Metaxa brandy. Slice enough tongue for four, place with the sauce in a shallow casserole, and warm everything together in a moderate 325° oven. This is something to devour slowly in a general purpose room, such as our log cabin, where meditative book shelves lend their own patterns of haphazardly mixed hues.

CARIBOU HEART

Cut out the coarse blood vessels in the top and interior of the heart. Wipe dry. Mix a cup of fine, dry bread or bannock crumbs, 1 small diced onion, 1/2 teaspoon salt, 1/4 teaspoon apiece of thyme and sweet basil and marjoram, 1/8 teaspoon freshly ground black pepper, and 3 teaspoons melted butter or margarine. Fill the cavity with this.

Set on rack in roaster. Pour a cup of boiling water into the bottom of the pan. Cover, set in a moderate 325° oven, and bake 3 hours or until tender. The results will form a pleasant background to the clatter of coffee cups and conversation.

BRAISED CARIBOU

Later in the season, when the meat is lean, lard a 4-pound caribou roast with chilled bacon cut into 1/4-inch strips, doing this either with a larding needle or by pressing them through slits cut in the meat at right angles to the grain; this so that the caribou can later be most advantageously sliced. Rub the outside of the meat liberally with butter or margarine, then with a teaspoon of garlic salt and 1/8 teaspoon lemon pepper.

Brown the meat thoroughly in 2 tablespoons cooking oil or, better, rendered bear lard, in which you've just browned 1/2 cup sliced onion. Using a Dutch oven, simmer with a cup of boiling water either atop the stove over low heat or in a moderate 325° oven for 2 hours or until tender, adding more water from time to time if necessary.

At the very end, saute a pound of sliced mushrooms in 2 tablespoons of butter or margarine in a frypan over low heat for 5 minutes, frequently stirring. Add to the braised caribou. Somehow this is an intimate dish more suitable for a luncheon with close friends on the lawn than for a formal dinner.

BOILED CARIBOU

You may not agree until you've had a season to test it for yourself, but when one has to eat his eay through a lot of caribou or other venison, boiling becomes the favorite way of preparation.

Cut a 4-pound chunk that will fit one of your pots rather snugly at the sides. Cover it with boiling water and bring the water to a boil once more. Spoon off the rising fat and scum.

Add a large sliced onion, a large sliced carrot, a sliced stalk of celery, 1/2 teaspoon freshly ground black pepper, and salt to taste. Simmer 3 hours or until the meat is fork tender. Drain the broth and save for future use or for sipping hot with the sliced meat and boiled potatoes. The whole will be as memorable as the sight, after a storm, of moonbeams in a cloud-heightened sky.

CARIBOU RIB ROAST

Cut off about a 4-pound rib roast. Rub well with 2 tablespoons of soft butter or margarine. Then sprinkle on 1/2 teaspoon salt, 1/8 teaspoon freshly ground black pepper, and 1/8 teaspoon paprika. Set on a rack in a roasting pan in a preheated moderate 350° oven and cook, uncovered, for 50 minutes or until tender.

If you see shortly before the roast is done that there is not going to be enough juice for gravy, add hot water to the bottom of the pan. Then, once the meat is done and removed to a warm spot, take out the rack. Mix 1 tablespoon of flour to a paste with a little water and add slowly to the liquid, stirring to prevent lumping. A bit more flour and water can be mixed in to give the gravy a desirable consistency. Adjust the seasoning and simmer 3 minutes or until the raw taste is gone from the flour. Such a roast has what some scholars might call panache.

CARIBOU LIVER

If the hunting has been as good as it can be with caribou and you've a lot of liver to eat your way through, for a change of pace slice about a 1 1/2-pound portion of this dark meat very thin. Then, using a sharp knife and a carving board, cut the liver across into very thin, matchlike pieces.

Saute half a dozen, medium-size, thinly sliced onions in 1/2 stick of margarine or butter in the frypan until the onions, softening, become temptingly tan. Then, stirring, saute the liver for 2 minutes, only until it loses its redness. Season to taste with salt, freshly ground black pepper, and parsley flakes. Serve with hot baking powder biscuits. Liver cooked this way is as intriguing as a Coptic sentence.

ELK FILLETS

When you've exhausted your usual ways of dealing with a freezer-load of elk, especially when the meat is a little off flavor, here's a way of handling it that will give fresh verve to your meals. Cut 2 pounds of inch-wide strips from a quarter, shorten them to about 4 inches in length, and flatten them by pounding.

Blend 1/2 cup of oil, 1/2 cup of good dry red wine, a large chopped onion, a crushed clove of garlic, 2 tablespoons lemon juice, 1 teaspoon salt, and 1/2 teaspoon freshly ground black pepper. Add the meat, cover, and refrigerate half a day, stirring from the bottom up from time to time.

When you're ready to eat, melt 1/4 stick of butter or margarine in your heavy frypan, sear the fillets on both sides, then lower the heat and saute them until tender. Stir 1/4 cup of your favorite Spanish-style tomato sauce into the marinade, add to the meat, bring to a simmer for 3 minutes, and serve. It will prove that whom the gods would elate, they first make hungry.

Try these fillets with hot garlic bread made by slicing a long French loaf in half lengthwise and drenching the cut sides with a stick of melted butter or margarine in which a crushed clove of garlic has been simmered for a dozen minutes, over heat so low that the spread does not brown. Sprinkle with 1/2 teaspoon chopped parsley and 1/4 teaspoon paprika. Heat the bread throughout in a moderate 325° oven, cut into thick slices, and serve inside a napkin in a long slim basket. The whole thing adds up into a hungry man's dish, not difficult enough to harass even the most harried cook.

ELK MEAT LOAF

When you're eating your way through an elk or two, the following meat loaf will provide such a sumptuous change of pace that you may elect to use it with the tougher parts of other venison. With the 2 pounds of ground elk you'll need to feed four, I like to grind in 2/3 pound of beef fat.

Then mix well with 2 cups of bread crumbs that have been slightly moistened with elk broth or beef bouillon, 1/2 cup grated onion, 2 tablespoons lemon juice, 2 teaspoons salt, and 1/4 teaspoon each of freshly ground black pepper, cinnamon, and allspice. Bind together with 6 beaten egg yolks and pack in a well-greased casserole or pan.

Now melt 2 tablespoons of butter or margarine. Mix separately 3 tablespoons flour, 1/4 teaspoon salt, and 1/8 teaspoon pepper. Add gradually to the melted grease, stirring constantly.

Slowly, all the time stirring, add a cup of elk or beef broth. Bring to a bubble and simmer for 3 minutes, then stir in 2 more tablespoons of flour that have first been smoothly mixed to a thin paste with a little cold water.

Bring to a simmer 2 cups of grated onions in just enough water to cover and cook 6 minutes. Drain. Then cover with boiling water and simmer until soft. Drain, press through a sieve, and mix with the sauce. Pour this sauce over the elk loaf, dust with paprika and parsley flakes, and bake in a moderate 350° oven an hour. The result will be as pretty as a new stamp; this ticket to somewhere, in this case a journey to gastronomical delight.

ELK GOULASH

Dice 3 pounds of the toughest part of the animal. Dredge in 2 tablespoons flour, 3 teaspoons paprika, 1 teaspoon salt, and 1/4 teaspoon freshly ground black pepper. Then brown along with 3 cups diced onions in 1/2 stick of butter or margarine and 1 tablespoon of cooking oil.

Add 2 cups diced potatoes, a sliced clove of garlic. Pour in a cup of beef bouillon, cover tightly, and simmer until the elk is tender, adding a bit of water if necessary. Adjust the salt and serve. Such a goulash is as exciting as a new map.

ELK CURRY

If you're ever visiting the native markets in southern Africa and Asia, you've no doubt marveled at the colorful mounds of various curries with provocative names, made with different strengths and combinations of spices. On this continent you usually have to settle for what you like best among the packaged brands. The only thing? Get your curry in small quantities and use it when it is as fresh as possible. We just had some more last night, with the inevitable chutney, so it is with feeling that I am suggesting the following recipe.

Start by trimming 2 1/2 pounds of elk rump and cutting it into 1/2-inch strips. Heat 3 tablespoons vegetable oil. Stir in 2 medium-size chopped onions, 2 teaspoons curry powder, 1 clove crushed garlic, 1/8 teaspoon chili powder, and if you have it 1/8 teaspoon saffron. Now lay in the meat and, stirring, brown it well.

Put in 1 cup beef bouillon and 2 tablespoons soy sauce. Simmer, covered, for 1/2 hour or until the meat is tender. Serve over steaming white rice, and let each guest bedeck his portion according to his individual tastes from small dishes of ground peanuts, minced hard-boiled egg, chopped onion, steamed white seedless raisins, and chopped crystallized ginger. Just as chess is a variation of an ancient East Indian game, so does this wild-game dish have a foreign origin intriguingly shrouded in mystery.

HUNTER'S PIE

I've enjoyed this particularly with elk when there has been enough cold roast left over to give us 4 cups of chopped meat. You also use a similar amount of mashed potatoes seasoned to taste with freshly ground pepper, salt, and paprika.

Thinly slice 2 onions and 2 cooking apples. Mix 2 egg yolks with the potatoes, then fold in the fluffily beaten whites. Cover the bottom of a baking dish with a thick layer of the thus embellished potatoes. Then spoon in layers of the chopped meat that has been salted and peppered to taste, onions and apple, and more potatoes in that order, ending up with a spreading of potatoes.

Pour on a cup of elk broth or gravy. Dot with butter or margarine. Sprinkle on shredded mozzarella cheese blended with Romano and Parmesan, paprika, and parsley flakes. Bake in a moderate 350° oven 1 hour. The results will be as homey as the squeak of your grandparents' pump and the wooden rattle of a bucket.

ELK SAUERBRATEN

You'll need 4 pounds of boneless meat cut from a hind quarter. Make a brine for this by mixing 2 cups water and 2 cups of vinegar with a large sliced onion, a dozen peppercorns, 1 sliced carrot, 4 tablespoons salt, 1 tablespoon whole cloves, 1 tablespoon whole mustard seeds, and 1 teaspoon whole celery seeds. Pickle the meat in this in a deep enamel, stainless steel, glass, or earthenware container for 4 days, turning it morning and night.

Saving the brine, transfer the meat, swabbed with 3 tablespoons butter or margarine, to a roasting pan and roast it in a slow 300° oven for 2 hours, whereupon the elk should be well tanned on all sides and nearly tender enough to eat. If it seems to be drying out too rapidly during the roasting process, baste with the brine.

Then sprinkle 3 tablespoons of brown sugar over the meat and roast it 10 minutes more or until the dissolving sugar has turned it appetizingly bronze.

Mix 1/4 cup flour into a smooth paste with a little water and stir slowly into the remaining brine, along with 4 crumbled gingersnaps. Cascade over the elk and roast another 1/2 hour or until the liquid is thick and smooth. Fork out the meat. Stir 1/2 cup Burgundy into the gravy. Then skim the grease from it, strain, and serve with the meat and steaming hot noodles. This is just the thing for a cool Sunday evening when church bells, long since stopped pealing, are still a vibration in your memory.

BROILED BISON

Steaks from young buffalo are tender, fine-grained, and similar in taste and appearance to choice beef although slightly heavier and somewhat darker. They're delicious broiled, particularly if you'll take them out of the refrigerator about an hour before cooking and let them reach room temperature. Preheat the oven about 8 minutes and grease the rack beforehand by rubbing it with a bit of fat, perhaps some of the excellent suet that surrounds the bison kidneys. Place a pan underneath to catch the juices which, when all is done, you'll spoon over the meat.

Cut the 4 steaks about 1 1/2 inches thick, allowing about 3/4 pound per diner. Cook about 7 minutes a side, some 5 inches below the heating element. If the steak is thicker, increase this distance. Then turn and cook the same length of time on the other side.

Gashing or pricking the meat is the best way to test for doneness. If red blood wells forth, the steak is rare. If the juice is pink, the meat is medium rare. Colorless? It's overdone unless that is the way someone prefers it.

At the end when you've removed the steaks to a hot platter and spooned the juices over them, dot with daubs of butter or margarine and sprinkle with freshly ground black pepper and salt to taste. It'll be like an evening out of a travel folder.

BUFFALO HUMP

With buffalo now legal game around the Northwest Territories, Great Slave Lake, and occasionally in Alaska, and with surplus bison regularly being harvested in other places in both countries, buffalo hump is again being relished by more and more North Americans.

When I can come by a substantial chunk, with its characteristic streaks or orangish fat, I like to salt it lightly, then ease it into a moderate 350° oven, with the fattest portion uppermost, to roast slowly, uncovered, while basting itself to a turn. This is much too fine fare, many of us reckon, to serve any other way but rare.

To spread appetizingly across it, cream a stick of butter or margarine with a teaspoon of chopped green onion, a teaspoon lemon juice, a teaspoon dill, a teaspoon paprika, 1/2 teaspoon seasoned salt, 1/2 teaspoon parsley flakes, 1/4 teaspoon freshly ground black pepper, and the juice of a crushed clove of garlic. The results will be as sprightly as a minuet.

BUFFALO A LA MODE

When you're hunting for a trophy and your buffalo is four years old or even more venerable, it's time to take moist-cooking methods into account. One of the more successful of these requires a 4-pound chunk of round or rump, larded unless there is already some fat on it.

Place in a deep stainless steel, pottery, or glass bowl with 2 cups Burgundy, 1 tablespoon salt, 1 teaspoon apiece of thyme and marjoram and cloves, 1/2 teaspoon freshly ground black pepper, 4 medium-size sliced onions, 3 medium-size sliced carrots, and a small sliced stalk of celery with the leaves. Prepare one afternoon and let it stand, covered, until the next.

Then fork out the meat and dry it with paper towels. Strain the liquid.

Warm a Dutch oven over high heat, swiping it liberally with bison or beef fat. Then brown the meat thoroughly.

Keep it off the bottom afterwards with a rack or such so that it will not stick, pour on the strained liquid, cover, lower the heat, and simmer very slowly for three hours or until a testing fork proves it to be tender. Have at least an inch of liquid in the bottom throughout, adding more Burgundy if this should become necessary.

Once the buffalo is tender, remove it and the fluid separately from the pot. Skim the fat off the juices. Taste and if necessary adjust the salt. Then return the meat and the juices to the Dutch oven and, basting, cook very slowly another 15 minutes. Have enough sliced carrots and tiny onions for dinner all cooked. Add these, hot, to the Dutch oven the last 5 minutes. Serve, streaming with the dark gravy. There's a quality of serene timelessness to such a meal, as though somehow it is hitched neither to the past nor the future.

BUFFALO AND BURGUNDY

Dice 4 strips of smoked bacon or the equivalent of buffalo kidney fat. Place in a deep, heavy frypan along with a dozen small, white onions. Heat and stir until the onions are golden. Then remove the onions for the time being.

Add 2 pounds of meat from one of the quarters, cut into 1-inch cubes, and brown in the grease. Stirring, add 2 tablespoons flour, 1 teaspoon salt, 1 teaspoon parsley flakes, 1/2 teaspoon thyme, 1/2 teaspoon marjoram, 1/2 teaspoon paprika, and a crushed clove of garlic. Then pour in a cup of Burgundy and another of beef bouillon. Cover and cook in a slow 350° oven for 4 hours.

Return the onions, add 8 small peeled potatoes, and a cup of sliced mushrooms. Cook another 20 minutes or until the potatoes are tender. Correct the salt if necessary, garnish with watercress, and serve. This is something when you're watching a northern sunset flower into a warm, red-petalled sky.

BRAISED BUFFALO SHORT RIBS

Cut about 4 pounds of plump, meaty bison ribs into serving sizes. Dredge in flour. In a deep frypan or a Dutch oven, brown on all sides, keeping all but a small amount of the grease poured off. Then add a cup of beef bouillon, along with 1/2 teaspoon thyme, 1/4 teaspoon marjoram, and garlic salt to taste. Cover and cook slowly in a moderate 325° oven for 2 hours or until tender. All your doubts at cooking something so new and different will be gone as soon as everyone digs in enthusiastically.

BUFFALO RIB ROAST

Bone, roll, and tie a 4-pound chunk of this tender meat. Roll in flour. In a Dutch oven atop the stove, brown the section of buffalo thoroughly in 1/2 stick of melted butter or margarine.

Add a cup of diced onion, 1/2 cup diced carrot, the contents of a small can of sliced mushrooms, and a minced clove of garlic. Saute until these, too, are brown.

Pour in 2 cups dry Burgundy, 1/2 teaspoon lemon pepper, 1/4 teaspoon thyme, 1/4 teaspoon marjoram, and salt to taste. Cover and bake some 3 hours in a moderate 325°oven or until the meat is fork tender, adding more wine if necessary. Shift the roast to a hot platter. Then strain the liquid, adjust its seasoning, and pour atop the buffalo which will be supreme.

WILD BOAR SCRAPPLE

There's boar hunting just up the Pacific Coast from where we spend part of our time among the hillside pines of

Cambria, California, and when Colonel Townsend Whelen, long the dean of the outdoor writers, was stationed in Monterey he enjoyed it, too. The Colonel was born and brought up in Philadelphia, and his recipe for scrapple comes from there.

Colonel Whelen preferred to remove the eyes and tongue from the head of a wild boar, then boil it in enough water barely to cover until the meat comes off the bones. Add 1 teaspoon salt and 1/4 teaspoon freshly ground black pepper along toward the end. Remove the meat from the stock and let both cool, skimming most of the grease off the stock. Then strain the stock.

However, if you prefer, you can simmer 3 pounds of fresh boar shoulder in 2 quarts of water, starting the meat in both instances in cold water. Add 1 teaspoon salt and 1/4 teaspoon pepper when the shoulder is nearly done. Then remove the meat from the stock and shred with a fork. Skim off the grease before straining the stock. Let 2 cups of this liquid cool. Continue to simmer 5 cups of it, now in the upper part of a double boiler.

Mix 2 pounds of cornmeal for every 3 pounds of meat. Bit by bit add the 2 cups of cooled stock to the cornmeal, stirring all the while to blend it into a velvety paste. Dribble this into the simmering stock, stirring constantly.

Add 1/2 teaspoon salt, 1/4 teaspoon freshly ground black pepper, and a tablespoon of onion juice. Then put in the shredded meat and cook in the top of the double boiler for an hour. Afterwards, pour the results into a greased enamel or stainless steel pan and let cool. Adjust the seasoning at this time.

When the scrapple is cool, cut the loaf into slices about 1/3 inch thick and fry until brown in a little bacon fat. Serve very hot, with maple syrup if you like. Summed the Colonel, "I had scrapple for breakfast twice a week for the first 21 years of my life. Fine grub!"

BOAR SADDLE

Rub the saddle with 2 tablespoons lemon juice, a clove of minced garlic, 1 teaspoon salt, 1 teaspoon thyme, and 1/4 teaspoon freshly ground black pepper. Place, fat side up, on a rack in an open roasting pan in a preheated moderate 350° oven. Roast 40 minutes a pound, basting frequently with the drippings.

If the saddle is not plump—and the rich, red meat that results from a diet of wild nuts and roots is frequently lean—bard it with pork fat.

When the saddle is done, remove it to a hot platter and spoon off most of the fat from the roaster. Pour in ¼ cup boiling water. Stir, loosening the brown glaze and adding its tastiness to the gravy. Simmer until well blended, seasoning to taste, and thin with more boiling water if you so desire. Serve over the roast that has been surrounded with hot slices of sweet potato. This is just the sort of meal to mingle its smells with the land's bittersweetness of fall, the wood smoke and the drying leaves, and the sharpness of juniper crushed underfoot.

STUFFED BOAR CHOPS

Place 4 big lean chops in a large, heavy frypan with almost enough water to cover. Salt and pepper to taste. Cover tightly and simmer 30 minutes. Then pour off the water.

Spread 2 tablespoons of raw, washed rice atop each chop. Then pile on a slice of tomato, a slice of onion, and a slice of green pepper. Pour in enough water almost to cover the rice. Cover and cook another 1/2 hour or until the meat is tender. Sprinkle with paprika and serve. Such chops are something to be pleasurably anticipated, like an unread book.

BAKED BOAR CHOPS

Season 4 loin chops, cut about 2 inches thick, to taste with salt and freshly ground black pepper, then dredge in flour. Melt 1/2 stick butter or margarine in a heavy frypan and brown the chops on both sides. Then remove the meat to a baking pan.

Stir 1/2 cup sour cream, 1/2 cup water, 2 tablespoons vinegar, 2 teaspoons sugar, and 2 teaspoons summer savory into the drippings in the frypan. Bring to a bubble and cascade over the chops. Cover and bake in a moderate 325° oven 1 3/4 hours. All you need to go with this is the small, steady creak of your grandmother's rocker.

BOAR STEAKS

Brown the steaks on both sides in a heavy frypan, then tip out any fat. Salt and pepper to taste. Cover with chicken consomme. Add a chopped onion and 1/8 teaspoon marjoram. Put the lid on tightly and cook slowly about 1 1/2 hours or until very tender. Serve with hot applesauce. These will bring back the old thoughts of your first hunt, of the excitement and the great atavistic content afterward.

BOAR TENDERLOIN

You'll need about 2 pounds to serve four. Cut 1/2-inch-thick slices, then flatten them to half that width by pounding them with the side of a cleaver, the back of a heavy knife, or even the rim of a staunch plate. Rub with a halved clove of garlic. Then brush with a mixture of 3 tablespoons melted butter or margarine, 1 teaspoon lemon juice, and 1 teaspoon of the juice of a crushed onion.

Heat a heavy frypan until when a few drops of cold water are scattered into it, they bounce to dryness almost immediately. Brown the meat on both sides, then lower the heat and pan broil slowly 1/2 hour or until thoroughly done. Salt, pepper, dust with parsley flakes, and serve. When you first taste this, your last doubts will whirlpool away like clear running water out of a porcelain sink.

SAVORY ANTELOPE ROAST

Because pronghorns as a whole are somewhat gamier than deer, you may choose to insert slivers of garlic in inch-deep slits cut in the sides of your 4-pound roast. Rub with 1 1/4 teaspoons salt and 1/4 teaspoon freshly ground black pepper. Dredge with flour.

Heat 2 tablespoons of butter or margarine and 1 tablespoon vegetable oil in your Dutch oven and brown the meat on all sides, along with 1/4 cup chopped onion. Add a can of condensed mushroom soup and a large can, juice and all, of sliced mushrooms. Roast covered, in a moderate 325° oven 2 1/2 hours or until fork tender, while the evening stretches about you, its stillness absorbing the sputterings of the meat.

ANTELOPE CUTLETS IN SOUR CREAM

Cut your slices 1/2-inch thick from an antelope hind quarter. For some 2 pounds of these, enough to serve four, melt a stick of butter or margarine in a heavy frypan. Rub proportionately 1 teaspoon salt and 1/8 teaspoon freshly ground black pepper into the cutlets, then dust well with flour. Brown on both sides over low heat.

Then pour 2 cups of sour cream over the meat. Simmer until just tender. Shake on paprika and parsley flakes for added taste, nourishment, and color. Serve with steaming buttered spaghetti emphasizing the delicate flavor.

ROAST ANTELOPE SADDLE

Sprinkle the saddle with proportionately 1 teaspoon salt and 1/8 teaspoon freshly ground black pepper and rub in well. Unless the pronghorn is fat, lay strips of salt pork across the top for basting. Place on a rack in an open roaster. Set in a preheated 350° oven and cook 15 minutes a pound or until the roast is done to your satisfaction.

For the gravy, transfer the juices to a saucepan over moderate heat. If you can see there is not going to be sufficient liquid, add a bit of hot water shortly before the roast is done. Mix a tablespoon of flour in a little water, stirring thoroughly until you have a smooth paste. Add to the liquid in the pan, stirring all the while to prevent lumping. If the gravy is still not sufficiently thick, add a little more flour and water in the same manner. Cook until the flour loses its raw taste.

The slices from this sputtering gravy-drenched saddle will be good with a wine jelly.

For special occasions, substitute chestnut Madeira for the gravy. For four, you'll need a pound of chestnuts. Using a sharp knife, gash an X on the flat side of each nut. Coat the batch with a tablespoon of olive oil, place in a flat pan, and bake in a moderate 375° oven for 1/4 hour. After cooling, remove the shells and inner skins. Glaze by heating very slowly in a frypan for a dozen minutes in a mixture of a tablespoon of beef bouillon paste and 2 tablespoons water.

Now saute 1 1/2 tablespoons grated onion in a frypan with a tablespoon of butter or margarine until the bits are soft and lightly tanned. Add 1/3 cup beef bouillon and simmer until the sauce is reduced by half. Stir in 3 tablespoons Madeira, add the chestnut mixture, bring to a bubble, and serve with the hot antelope.

SMOTHERED MOUNTAIN GOAT

Mountain goat, particularly if you're gunning for a

trophy, is apt to be darker, stronger, and tougher than what you might expect, but the following recipe quells the meat deliciously. Start it by cutting 2 pounds of 1-inch cubes. Roll these in 1/2 cup flour, 1 teaspoon salt, and 1/8 teaspoon freshly ground black pepper.

Stirring, cook 1 1/2 cups of chopped onion in 1/4 cup vegetable oil until tender. Then add the cubes and brown both them and the vegetable.

Slowly add 1 cup of sour cream—or if you're camping, 1 cup of evaporated milk and 1 tablespoon mild vinegar—all the time stirring. Then mix in 2 1/2 tablespoons grated cheese. Put on the lid and simmer for 2 hours, adding boiling water if the mixture seems to be becoming dry. Adjust the seasoning, dust with paprika, and serve over hot, sectioned boiled potatoes. The results will be as fetching as a scale model of a 1926 Three-litre Bentley.

MARINATED MOUNTAIN GOAT RIBS

Saw 4 pounds of short ribs into serving portions. Spread flat over the bottom of a large pan.

In a separate pot mix 2 cups chopped onions, an 8-ounce can of tomato sauce, 1 cup concentrated beef bouillon, 1 tablespoon Worcestershire sauce, 1 tablespoon prepared horseradish, 2 teaspoons sugar, 1 teaspoon apiece of wine vinegar, salt, and dry mustard, and 1/8 teaspoon freshly ground black pepper. Bring to a bubble for 10 minutes.

Pour hot over the meat. Marinate for 8 hours, turning several times.

Then shift the ribs and the marinade to a Dutch oven, cover, and simmer for 3 hours or until tender, spooning the marinade over the meat occasionally. When you eat this after a hard day, you'll find it'll win your attention far more than any great-restaurant masterpiece that holds no memories.

MOUNTAIN SHEEP

I can't improve on what I've said in the past about mountain sheep which, in addition to being the hardest-won and most-highly prized of this continent's big game trophies, provides the closest you're ever likely to come to true gourmet dining among the wild meats of this earth.

This supremely surpassing game is prepared like the choicest venison, although few will settle for anything's encroaching upon its superlative natural savor but salt, butter or the best margarine, and possibly a dusting of newly ground black pepper. And when you're turning the last odds and ends into stews, it's best for this reason to confine these to the blander vegetables such as potatoes, carrots, and peas.

The dark green, square-stemmed mint [*Mentha*] that often thrives nearby, however, can subtly point up the ambrosial flavor of a large rare roast. You can make a discreet sauce of this by warming 1/2 cup mild vinegar, 1/3 cup white sugar, and 1/4 teaspoon salt. Stir in finely chopped young mint leaves to taste, about 1/3 cup, and let the portion cool before serving. But even such a companionable wild mint adjunct, you'll likely agree, should be employed frugally with this king of the epicurean repasts.

BIG GAME HASH

I can't suggest a better big game hash than I describe in what in the paperback edition is my *Good Food From The Woods*. Any big game will do. For a really splendiferous taste, especially if you help matters along with the distinctive flavors of wild greens, begin by dicing 2 large onions, then sauteing them in 1/2 stick of butter or margarine until they are soft but not brown.

Then tan 2 cups of diced, freshly boiled potatoes in the same pan with onions. Add 1/2 cup of cooked, well drained, cut-up greens such as dandelions or mustard and stir this around a bit. Two cups of diced, cooked game meat go in next.

Moisten all this with 1/2 cup of stock from the meat or vegetables, seasoned with a crushed garlic clove, a teaspoon of salt, 1/2 teaspoon ginger, 1/4 teaspoon monosodium glutamate, and 1/8 teaspoon freshly ground black pepper.

Arrange in a pan in the shape of an omelet. Bake in a moderate 350° oven for 15 minutes. Then scatter some chips of butter or margarine on top and finish by browning under the broiler. You can almost hear the creaking wheels of covered wagon trains when you eat grub like this.

MARROW

The mineral-and-vitamin-rich marrow found in the bones of big game that was in good condition when it was bagged is not equaled in nourishment by any other natural food. What is also the most succulent of morsels is depleted by overcooking, however. Saw the large marrowbones into convenient lengths of from about 4 to 6 inches. Either simmer in water for 10 minutes or roast in a moderate 350° oven 1/2 hour.

Unless you are already armed with the once more popular marrow forks or scoops, push out the soft vascular tissue with slim knives or with thin wooden sticks, blunt on one end. We enjoy this choicest of food as is, although you can salt and pepper it if you want and spread it on thin hot toast.

JERKY

The simplest way to preserve meat is by drying it. When this is done most advantageously, it's also one of the most delicious methods. If you've any doubts, try some of the beef jerky that is available in many markets and delicatessens. And note the price. The amount charged for several slim, blackened strips of this dehydrated meat will often buy a good steak.

There's nothing complicated about making jerky. You cut fat-trimmed deer, moose, elk, antelope, caribou, buffalo, and similar lean red meat into long straps about 1/2 inch thick. These you hang apart from one another in the sun, in the attic, or some other place where, kept well ventilated and dry, they will gradually lose most of their water content. At the same time they'll become hard, dry, black, and incidentally, both concentratedly nourishing and tasty.

The fresh strips can first be soaked, if you want, either in brine or sea water. If you are along the sea coast, you may care to try the ancient method of boiling down ocean water until it becomes extremely salty. While it is still bubbling, immerse a few strips at a time for 3 minutes apiece. If there is no convenient place to hang this meat, it can be laid across sun-warmed rocks and turned every hour or so. You can also make your own saturated brine by dissolving all the salt possible in boiling water.

After the meat has been permitted to drain, some makers dust it with black pepper. In many cases they also add favorite spices such as oregano, marjoram, basil, and thyme for increased flavor. Good? Ranch friends of ours in California and New Mexico, with plenty of space in their walk-in freezers, jerk a deer or two each year in this fashion just for their own personal snacking.

A common inland technique for jerking game meat involves draping the strips, or suspending them by wire or string loops, on a makeshift wooden framework about 4 to

6 feet off the ground. A small, slow, smoky fire of any nonresinous wood is built beneath this rack. The meat is allowed to dry for several days in the sun and wind. It is covered at night and during any rain. The major use of the fire is to discourage flies and other insects. It should not be hot enough to cook the meat at all.

When jerked, the meat will be hard and more or less black outside. It will keep almost indefinitely away from damp and flies. This covered-wagon staple is best eaten as is. It is very concentrated and nourishing, and a little goes a long way as an emergency ration. Alone, it is not a good food for long-continued consumption by itself, as it lacks the necessary fat.

All fat, which would turn rancid anyway, should be trimmed off before the drying operation commences. It can then be rendered for future use in cooking or in the manufacture of pemmican.

GENUINE PEMMICAN

Some frightful concoctions appear on the market from time to time under the misleading name of "pemmican," a Cree word for an Indian-manufactured trail food which is still the best natural concentrated rations ever. To get any real pemmican through normal channels today, though, you pretty much have to make your own.

Start by pounding up a quantity of jerky. Then take raw animal fat and cut it into walnut-size chunks. Fry these out in an open pan in the oven or over a slow fire, never letting the grease reach the boiling stage. Pour the resulting hot fat over the shredded jerky, mixing the two together until it is about the consistency of ordinary sausage. Then pack the pemmican in commercial casings or waterproof bags. Despite some practices, no salt at all should be included. Dried berries, an Indian practice? Suit yourself. Their function is for flavoring only.

The ideal proportions of lean and fat in pemmican is, by weight, approximately equal amounts of well-dried lean meat and rendered fat. It takes roughly 5 pounds of fresh lean meat to make 1 pound of jerky suitable for pemmican.

Such genuine pemmican affords practically every necessary food element with the exception of Vitamin C. The average individual can get along without this vitamin for at least 2 months if in good health to begin with. Not only that, but supplementing this pemmican with some fresh food—for example, with just several fresh rose hips daily—will supply all the Vitamin C necessary to prevent any difficulty with scurvy over even an extended period.

chapter two

GAME BIRDS

DURING THE INTERVALS between flights, especially near the start of the season while the days are still balmy, waterfowl should be drawn without delay. So should any game bird for that matter. Otherwise, you are in for a disappointment. Cut from the breastbone to and around the vent, then remove the lungs, intestines, heart, gizzard, and liver, saving the latter trio unless shot has penetrated them. Wipe out the cavity as with a cloth kept wrung out in clean water, dry grass, or paper toweling. Take out the craw and windpipe.

Leave on the feathers, though, unless you're about to freeze or use the fowl. Either that or, as when you're going to keep them in the ordinary compartment of the refrigerator or ship in regular ice, encase each bird separately in a moistureproof bag. If you've ever tried to pluck a fowl that has been frozen and thawed, you'll appreciate why if possible the bird should never be frozen with the plumage intact. And you'll be sacrificing a considerable amount of moistness and flavor if you skin your mallard, canvasback, teal, partridge, pheasant, or such.

To prepare for the fire, disjoint the legs at the first joint above the feet and the wings at the joint closest to the body. Pull out the feathers, avoiding as much as possible tearing the skin by plucking them out downwards, in the direction they have been growing. Grip the remaining pinfeathers between a finger and the blade of a knife and yank them out. The bird will likely still need singeing, either in the flame of a gas range or by running it back and forth a few times through the flames from a twisted piece of heavy paper. Then, no matter what the defeathering process, cut out the oil sacs that are located on either side of the spine just above the tail.

You can save yourself a lot of time and trouble by melting, for a dozen duck say, 6 12-ounce cakes of paraffin in 3 gallons of water. Let this mixture cool to about 165° before using, for if it is too warm, the paraffin will have a tendency to slide off the fowl. Dip each bird slowly into the fluid so that a layer of wax coats the plumage. Do this three times, with intervals in between so that the paraffin will harden.

On the other hand, leave the bird in the kettle no longer than expedient, as excess heat does nothing for subsequent flavor. Incidentally, the wax is flammable, so be careful. Now strip off the sheet of plumage and paraffin, removing any remaining tiny feathers and down by scraping them away with a knife. Then cut off the head about an inch above the body. By conservatively removing the feathers from the mixture each time, the same wax can be used all season.

It's a good idea to tag your fowl with their ages before you pluck them, for the age of game birds is usually an important consideration when it comes to cooking. With young waterfowl, the tips of the outermost tail feathers end in a V-shaped notch. By fall, these feathers will have been nearly all moulted or lost and replaced by plumage with rounded or pointed tips. Therefore, if the bird you bag has even one V-tipped tail feather, it's a youngling. If the tops are rounded or pointed, it is apt to be an oldster, although particularly late in the season the possibility remains that it's a fully moulted youngster. Horny feet and beaks are signs of advanced age.

With wild turkey, there's a foolproof age test. If the ends of the tail feathers still stick out beyond the rest, you have a young bird. The spurs of older pheasants are glossy, dark, sharp, and often slightly curved. If the spurs are dull, light colored, relatively stubby, and perhaps cone shaped, you've a youngling.

Age doesn't matter so much when you're preparing the smaller upland game birds. But for interested cooks the soundest clues are to be found in the wings. With young foul, the tips of the outermost pair of feathers there are more pointed than the rest. But you've already cut these all off? Then press the breastbone. This part of the skeleton becomes more and more rigid with maturity. With most youngsters you can easily bend in the tip with a lightly investigating forefinger.

There are some exceptions to the above pre-cooking suggestions. The same Federal regulations that make it illegal to possess migratory waterfowl for more than 90 days after the close of the regular season provide that head, head plumage, and feet must remain intact during storage. There are also some provincial and state laws governing the transportation and storage of game birds that may need individual checking.

WILD SOUTHWEST DUCK

This adds piquancy to a large mallard or canvasback, stuffed with 1/2 cup chopped green onion, 1/4 cup celery leaves, a small red pepper pod, and a bay leaf. Lay 1/4 pound salt pork, sliced in 1/3-inch-thick strips, atop the bird. Place on a rack in a shallow pan and slide into a preheated moderate 350° oven for 2 1/2 hours or until a leg bone will swing easily back and forth. Remove the pork for the last 1/2 hour. Cut the bird into moist, tempting slices, discarding the stuffing, and arrange these on a hot platter.

Keep the meat hot while you are preparing the sauce by melting 2 tablespoons butter or margarine in a frypan and smoothly stirring in 2 tablespoons of flour which you have first turned into a thin paste with a little cold water. Then mix in a can of concentrated beef bouillon or 1 1/3 cups of double-strength beef broth, prepared with water and 3 bouillon cubes or the equivalent in powder or paste. Add 1/4 freshly squeezed orange juice, 2 tablespoons of good red wine, and a tablespoon of currant jelly.

Bring to a bubble over low heat, stirring until the sauce thickens. Season to taste with salt and monosodium glutamate, pour over the wild duck, serve, and be prepared for some more enthusiastic gunning the next day and the day following.

WILD DUCK ROASTED IN FOIL

When dishing up duck, figure on about one pound per diner. The following recipes, therefore, being for foursomes as are the others in this book, are based on young canvasback or plump mallard weighing some 2 pounds apiece. Then there are Eastern Canada's cannard noir or black duck, the pintail, teal, redhead, widgeon, and numerous others. When preparing stuffing, for example, figuring on from 1/2 to 1 pound per pound of dressed fowl, the following stuffing will be sufficient for 2 average mallard or smaller canvasback, 3 pintail, 4 wood duck, or 3 to 6 teal.

This recipe was so popular in my *Gourmet Cooking For Free* that I am repeating it here. For strips of steaming duck meat that will warm a hungry man's heart, you may want to wait until the end of the season so you may select the plumpest, primest birds available.

Place the gizzards and hearts, cut into small cubes, in a small saucepan. Pour over them the liquid from a can of mushroom stems and pieces, and simmer gently for 15 minutes. Meanwhile, melt 2 tablespoons of butter or margarine and saute the diced duck livers for 2 to 3 minutes. Combine the diced gizzards and hearts, the livers and the buttered mushroom liquid along with the reserved mushroom pieces. Season with 1 teaspoon salt, 1/4 teaspoon freshly ground pepper, 1/2 teaspoon thyme. Pour over 3 cups of crumbled day-old white bread and toss lightly with a fork to blend. The stuffing will appear rather dry, but the delectable juices produced by cooking the ducks in foil will moisten it to the proper extent.

Rub each duck liberally inside and out with butter or margarine; sprinkle with salt and a little ginger. Stuff the cavities lightly with the dressing, so that it will have room to expand during the cooking. Lay each duck on a large doubled rectangle of heavy-duty aluminum foil and wrap, crimping all edges tightly. Arrange on a shallow pan and ease into a preheated hot 400° oven. After 10 minutes, when the birds have begun to sputter, reduce the heat to a moderate 325° for 2 hours for the larger ducks, a corresponding shorter time for the wood duck or teal.

If you restrain yourself from unwrapping these fowl to brown them, you will be rewarded with moist birds swimming in juices. Serve a cupful of this with each portion so the diner can dip each forkful of steaming bird into its gratifying flavor. A watercress salad, dressed with wine vinegar and freshly ground black pepper and just a little oil, goes well with this duck, especially if a north wind is blowing gusts of snow against the windows like charges of chilled shot.

CASHEW-STUFFED WILD DUCK

We came back from Mocambique a year ago ago with several 5-pound tins of salted cashews, went duck hunting, and ended up with the following recipe for a couple of 2-pound fowl.

Mix a cup apiece of chopped cashews, minced onion, diced celery, and seedless raisins, and 4 cups of fresh bread crumbs with 1/4 teaspoon salt. Stir 1/2 cup scalded milk into 2 beaten eggs and combine with the dry mixture. Stuff the ducks, sewing or pinning the slits shut. Arrange in roaster, sprinkle with paprika, lay 3 slices bacon atop each duck, and roast uncovered in a moderate 350° oven for 15 to 20 minutes per pound or until tender.

The last 20 minutes, combine 1 cup tomato catsup and 1/2 cup each of chili sauce, Worcestershire sauce, and A-1 sauce. Baste the fowl with the result while they are finishing cooking. Slice and serve steaming hot, each slice garnished with parsley and freshly sliced orange and well moistened with the fat-skimmed sauce remaining in the pan. It'll be lyrically impelling.

ROAST WILD DUCK

Wipe the birds with a damp cloth but, as with all game, do not wash. Rub each of two 2-pound duck inside and out with a teaspoon of salt and 1/8 teaspoon freshly ground black pepper. Melt a stick of butter or margarine in a roasting pan and brown the duck on all sides atop the stove.

In the meantime, be squeezing the juice from 2 lemons. Grate the rind and soak this in a jigger of good dry sherry,

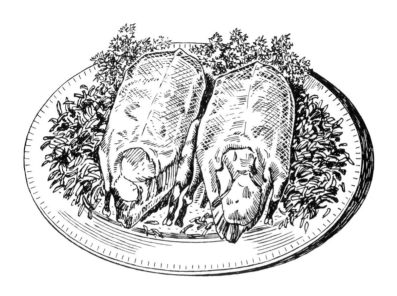

not so-called cooking sherry. Divide the lemon juice between the cavities of the 3 ducks. With a spoon, apply the rind and sherry to the sides. Roast uncovered in a slow 300° oven until the crisp skin and a prodding fork tell you they are tender and done. Serve on a hot platter, with the juices in the pan tipped over the fragrant meat. Your dining room will be suddenly warmer and snugger, and smelling of fruit and game and fresh white linen.

FOR A PROLONGED DIET OF ROAST WILD DUCK

Sometimes the gunning is so good, and the blinds so companionable, that you're in a position to enjoy duck night after night during the hunting season. Here's a recipe for roast duck that will let you do just that.

Rub the freshly wiped duck inside and out with a teaspoon of salt and 1/8 teaspoon freshly ground black pepper. To assist the flavor, place several small peeled onions, a scattering of tart apple slices, a bit of chopped celery, a sprig of parsley, 1/8 teaspoon marjoram, and 6 juniper berries inside each canvasback, mallard, black duck, or such. This filling is discarded after roasting. Skewer the opening.

Rub the bird liberally with soft butter or margarine. Place on a rack in a small uncovered pan. Heat the oven before setting in the fowl, its breast pinned with half a dozen strips of salt pork. Pour a blend of 1/2 cup claret and 1/2 cup water over it.

Roast at a very hot 500° for 15 minutes; a correspondingly briefer time if your duck is a pintail, teal, or one of the other smaller varieties. You'll discover that with the meat looking almost raw this way, you won't tire of roast duck even after sitting down to it day after day while the flights are settling in from the north. Basting every 5 minutes, at the same time brushing with fresh melted butter or margarine, will do much to sharpen both flavor and appetite.

Then whittle off all the meat and transfer in a pan to a warm spot. Using a duck press, crush the bones, mix the juices with the gravy, and pour over the meat. Touch up with fresh lemon juice, simmer until the blood sauce thickens, and serve flaming with warmed brandy.

Sportsmen argue about the heat at which duck can be most advantageously roasted. Perhaps you can answer this for your own particular palate if you'll also try one sometime in a moderate 325° oven for about 45 minutes.

DUCK IN BURGUNDY

Shake, several pieces at a time, about 4 pounds of disjointed and cut-up wild duck in a paper bag with 1/4 cup of flour seasoned to taste with freshly ground black pepper, salt, and paprika. Brown thoroughly in a frypan with 2 tablespoons of butter or margarine. Then arrange the meat in a buttered 3-quart casserole.

Saute in the grease remaining in the hot frypan 1/2 pound of sliced mushrooms and 3/4 cup chopped onion until the former have shriveled and the latter are soft. Now tilt the contents of the frypan into the casserole, tip in 2 cups of good dry Burgundy, stir, cover, and bake in a moderate 325° oven for 1 1/2 hours or until the fowl is fork tender.

Check the moisture content at this time, and if the casserole seems too dry, add boiling water. Stir in 3 cups of Minute Rice, a packet of frozen green peas, and 4 tablespoons of diced pimentos. Cover once more and resume baking for another 1/4 hour or until the peas are ready. The memory of duck prepared this way is poignant, like morning in an apple orchard.

WILD DUCK WITH ORANGE

For four diners, you'll want enough ducks to assure yourselves of about a pound of meat apiece. Dredge the birds with 1/4 cup flour, 1/2 teaspoon salt, and 1/8 teaspoon freshly ground black pepper. Place a sliced onion, later to be discarded, along with 1/8 teaspoon marjoram into the cavity of each. Chives with parsley will be even better.

Lay each duck on a large doubled rectangle of heavy-duty aluminum foil and wrap, allowing room for steam, crimping all edges securely. Arrange in a shallow pan and place in a preheated, hot 450° oven for 30 to 35 minutes, depending on the size of the duck.

Combine a cup of choice dry sherry, the juice and grated rind of a medium-size orange, 1 teaspoon cinnamon, and 1/4 teaspoon nutmeg and bring to a simmer. Five minutes before the ducks are ready to serve, open the top of the foil long enough to baste each fowl with 2 tablespoons of the sauce.

Keep the remainder of the sauce hot, and when you have gingerly shifted the ducks from foil to serving platter, pour it over the juicy, succulent repast.

SMOTHERED WILD DUCK

Cut each duck into half a dozen pieces. Saying you're dealing with 2-pound birds, rub each fowl with 1 teaspoon salt and 1/8 teaspoon freshly ground black pepper. Then roll in 1/2 cup flour. Get 1/2 cup of shortening (black bear lard is best) hot, just short of smoking, and fry the sections in it for 15 minutes a side, turning once.

Then pour in a cup of milk, cover tightly, and simmer slowly atop the stove for an hour or until tender. Better still, bake in a slow 300° oven until likewise tender. Sprinkle with parsley flakes and paprika and serve. The results will be as gentle and tender as a sated lover's thoughts.

PRESSED WILD DUCK

You'll need a fresh liver for each of the usual 2 ducks—more if they are the smaller teal or such—so if the regular duck livers were penetrated with shot or have overaged, substitute chicken livers which may be purchased frozen at most markets. Saute them 20 seconds a side in 3 tablespoons of hot butter or margarine, leaving them rare.

Then remove the livers and brown a tablespoon of flour in the grease, adding more of this latter if necessary. Drop in a tablespoon of diced onion and stir around until just tan. Then scatter on a dash of nutmeg, 1/8 teaspoon thyme, 1 teaspoon salt, 1/8 teaspoon freshly ground black pepper, 1 teaspoon Worcestershire sauce, and 1/4 cup dry claret.

Simmer 5 minutes, adding a bit of chicken broth, made with bouillon perhaps, if the mixture seems overthick. Now chop the livers, add these, and then mash everything through a sieve.

In the meantime, be roasting your ducks in a very hot 450° oven for 20 minutes, a correspondingly briefer time if they are pintail or another of the smaller varieties. Rub first with a teaspoon salt and 1/8 teaspoon freshly ground black pepper, then with a liberal amount of softened butter or margarine. Add 1/4 cup claret and 1/4 cup water to keep everything moist, and place on a rack on a small pan.

Then skin the breasts and slice them thinly. Extract juices from the remainder with a duck press and add this to the liver sauce, along with a jigger of Metaxa brandy. Bring this all to a simmer, turn the slices in the odiferous mixture, and serve on hot toast points or wild rice. This is good when the crickets are sounding their tiny autumn bells all around.

WILD DUCK WITH SAUERKRAUT

Split enough ducks for four servings—about 4 pounds. Commence the stove activities by warming 2 tablespoons of bacon drippings and 2 tablespoons shortening, short of smoking, in a deep cast-iron frypan. Chop 1/4 pound of preferably yellow onion and, stirring, simmer until soft and well tanned but not burned. Add a diced, unpeeled cooking apple, then 4 cups sauerkraut. Get everything hot.

In the meantime, rub the ducks inside and out with butter or margarine and with proportionately 1 teaspoon of salt to 1/8 teaspoon freshly ground black pepper. Sprinkle with paprika. Spread, hollow sides down, atop the steaming sauerkraut, onion, and apple bed. Cover, with a heavy-duty aluminum foil canopy if necessary. Cook slowly some 1 1/2 hours or until the meat is tender.

For a sweet-and-sour taste change on occasion, pour a 6-ounce can of concentrated orange juice and 1/4 cup water over the steaming sauerkraut at the start. Either way, the results will enhance an autumn bigger with snow.

RUMDUM ROAST WILD DUCK

Slice enough onions and oranges in equal proportions to stuff the cavities of sufficient ducks to feed four. Add a tablespoon of orange curacao to the interior of each bird. Rub the outsides of the fowl with butter or margarine and a diced clove of garlic.

Place the ducks, breasts upward, in a low uncovered pan in a preheated hot 450° oven until the tops are bronzed. Then reduce the heat to a moderate 350° and roast until tender, basting with the drippings and 2 jiggers of rum. Dust lightly with ginger before serving. This is particularly perfect for a blue September, smoky with falling leaves.

WILD DUCK PIE

This is good for those ducks of advanced or indeterminate age when you're spending a rainy, card-playing afternoon in camp with full bags and a cozy fire snapping in the stove. A large canvasback, a couple of medium-size black duck, or a quartet of teal or such will satisfy four boon companions.

Cut, disjointing whenever possible, into serving pieces. Brown these in 2 tablespoons each of butter or margarine and shortening in a large, cast-iron frypan. Then add 1 teaspoon salt, 1/8 teaspoon cayenne pepper, a bay leaf, a sprinkling of allspice, and a jigger of gin. Cover with water, bring to a bubble, and simmer an hour or until tender. Then bone the meat and shift it to a casserole.

Pour the stock into a saucepan, freeing the frypan for the sauteing of a cup of diced carrots, 1/4 cut chopped onions, and 3 tablespoons diced celery in 2 tablespoons apiece of butter or margarine and shortening until lightly tanned. Then add them to the stock, along with 2 cups of potatoes cut into 1/2-inch cubes, and simmer 20 minutes. Pour into the casserole.

Brown 3 tablespoons flour in the fat remaining in the frypan, add 3 cups stock borrowed from the casserole, and simmer until thickened. Season to taste with salt and freshly ground black pepper and 1 teaspoon Worcestershire sauce. Turn over the meat and vegetables.

A good crust can be made by carefully combining 1/6 cup of shortening with a cup of all-purpose flour, sifted with 1/2 teaspoon salt, until what you reach is about the same consistency as corn meal. Then add another 1/6 cup shortening and blend until the flour is completely absorbed, and you have a consistency like that of large peas.

Add by teaspoonfuls 2 to 3 tablespoons cold water, tossing lightly with a fork until the mixture is barely dampened. Gather into a ball in waxed paper, then chill. Finally, roll out on a plastic or other surface well dusted with the same type of flour, until it is about 1/8 inch thick. Place atop the casserole, allow 1/2-inch margin when you trim, gash to allow the escape of steam, and bake in a hot 450° oven about 15 minutes or until tan. Serve with cranberry sauce.

BROILED WILD DUCK

This becomes distinguished when imbued with the flavor of glowing charcoal, but even a regular broiler will make it sumptuous. Split your young ducks lengthwise, rub sparingly with salt and freshly ground black pepper, immerse with olive oil on a plate with the help of a spoon, and broil about a dozen minutes a side, turning as necessary to prevent charring.

Sprinkle with paprika and chopped parsley, pour on golden melted butter or margarine, and serve on a hot platter along with wedges of lemon.

CANTONESE DUCK

Mix in a large bowl 3/4 cup soy sauce, 2 tablespoons sherry, 4 finely chopped small onions, 2 stalks finely chopped celery, 1 tablespoon sugar, 2 cloves crushed garlic, 1 teaspoon powdered ginger, 1 teaspoon salt, 1/4 teaspoon monosodium glutamate, 1/8 teaspoon freshly ground black pepper, and 1 cup water.

Rub the 3 1/2 to 4-pound bird thoroughly with the mixture. Then pour the remainder into the fowl, sewing the opening tightly and tying the neck securely.

Place breast up on a rack in an open roasting pan. Cover the duck loosely with a piece of aluminum foil, not letting this touch the heating element if you are using an electric oven. Roast at a moderate 325° for about 3 hours or until a drumstick will move easily, removing the foil the last 1/2 hour so that the fowl will brown temptingly but not long enough to toughen it. Waiting for it to come out of the oven, you'll feel like one of Pavlov's salivating dogs for whom a bell has rung.

WILD GEESE

With only several differences, wild geese are handled the same way as duck. First, cut the large vein in the neck of the goose upon downing it and, if at all possible, hang by the feet to bleed. Second, because of the size, it will be more economical to pour the melted paraffin over the bird to defeather it instead of dipping it. Again, draw immediately after shooting for the best results, which can be very fine indeed, especially if you cook the fowl slowly for a long time and drain off the excess fat periodically.

Wild geese will be all the better if stuffed overnight with a sliced lemon and chopped onion as well as with perhaps some diced apple, laid in a covered roaster in a cool spot, after which these ingredients are removed.

After you've been shooting these giants awhile, you'll get in the habit of whenever possible selecting the last birds in the flight, as they're generally the youngest and tenderest.

ROAST YOUNG WILD GOOSE

This is for the tender fellows who weigh 8 pounds or less. Rub the bird inside and out with 4 parts salt and 1 part freshly ground black pepper. Stuff loosely with later-to-be-discarded slices of lemon and chopped onion, as well as some sliced apple if you have any. Truss. Crisscross the breast with slices of salt pork and lay additional slices over the wings and legs.

Or if you'd prefer a stuffing to eat, melt a stick of butter or margarine in a heavy frypan. Keeping the temperature short of smoking, stir around 1/2 cup of chopped onion until it is tan and tender. Then add 3 cups of soft bread crumbs, 1 cup of diced cooking apple, 1/2 cup chopped dried prunes and the same amount of chopped dried apricots, 1/2 teaspoon salt, 1/8 teaspoon freshly ground black pepper, and 1/8 teaspoon parsley flakes. Stuff the goose sparingly and either sew or pin the opening. Truss and add the salt pork slices as before.

In either event, place on back on a rack in an uncovered roasting pan and roast in a preheated slow 275° oven for some 35 minutes a pound until nearly tender, basting frequently and keeping the excess grease removed. As soon as the legs are loose and the bird is tan, remove the pork, raise the oven temperature to a moderate 350°, and bronze all over, basting with the pan juices once or twice during the necessary 10 or 15 minutes.

Gravy, the thing with which to spread subsequent sandwiches for any slices of goose remaining, can be prepared with the drippings and giblets.

WILD GOOSE AND WINE

This is best with a tender young goose weighing some 8 pounds or less, whereupon in the woods it will satisfactorily take care of Thanksgiving, either the Canadian or the American variety. Combine 1/2 stick of butter or margarine with 1/2 teaspoon salt, 1/2 teaspoon paprika, 1/2 teaspoon parsley flakes, 1/8 teaspoon freshly ground black pepper, and 1/8 teaspoon thyme. Rub the fowl generously with this mixture, inside and out.

Then fill the cavity with sliced cooking apples, 3 or 4 small onions, and a halved bulb of garlic. Lay on a large doubled rectangle of heavy-duty aluminum foil and bring this up around the sides. Pour on 2 cups of dry Burgundy. Then crimp the foil shut.

Arrange on a shallow pan and ease into a preheated hot 400° oven for 10 minutes. Then, when the bird has started to sputter, reduce the heat to a slow 275° for 2 to 3 hours or until the legs will move loosely. Then uncover long enough to brown. Remove the stuffing and serve with the juices covering the pieces of steaming meat and hot mashed potato, some of it seeping around ruddy slices of cold cranberry jelly.

ROAST OLDER WILD GOOSE

This is for the larger geese, weighing perhaps a dozen pounds or so, not for the real oldsters of the flock. The morning of the big event, stuff loosely with a mixture of 6 cups of dry bread crumbs, 3 cups chopped cooking apples, a cup of cooked chestnuts, a cup of sliced red onions, 1 tablespoon chopped parsley, and 1/2 teaspoon salt, all flavored with 1/2 cup Burgundy and mixed with 2 whipped eggs for substance. Sew or skewer the cavity and truss.

Blend a tablespoon of flour, another of sage, 1 teaspoon salt, 1 teaspoon paprika, 1/2 teaspoon freshly ground black pepper, and 1/2 teaspoon allspice. Rub into the goose, dusting the top with any that remains.

Set breast up in an uncovered roasting pan and slide into a preheated hot 400° oven for 15 minutes. Then reduce the heat to a slow 300° and roast until tender, whereupon the leg joints will move easily; a process that after the initial 1/2 hour will require about 20 minutes a pound. Keep accumulating grease removed.

For a really delicious bird, try to baste every dozen minutes with the drippings and a blended cup apiece of Burgundy and cider. There's rapture in such a goose.

OLD WILD GOOSE CASSEROLE

There's nothing like showing some respect for age, and this applies admirably to an aged honker, to repeat another of the more popular recipes of my *Gourmet Cooking For Free.* You'll spot him by his thick, coarse plumage and heavy, long-exercised spurs. No oven-roasting for this old-timer. After being hung for a bit, the bird should be simmered in a savory broth under tender, then used in a change-of-pace casserole.

Just cut the most readily available meat into strips, using the remainder for soup. Brown the meat in a frypan with a stick of butter or margarine, seasoning it to taste with salt and freshly ground black pepper.

In the meantime, start the cleaned and diced heart and gizzard simmering for 1/2 hour in a cup of white wine, 1/8 teaspoon celery seed, and salt and pepper to taste.

When the meat is browned, move it to a well-greased casserole. Remove the cooked heart and gizzard to the hot frypan, reserving the liquid in which they were cooked. Stir them around in the grease until the bits are bronzed. Pour in the liquid and stir vigorously over moderate heat to loosen all the browned particles in the frypan. Then pour everything into the waiting casserole. Add a dozen tiny onions and a cup of shredded carrots. Stir in sour cream to cover and set in a slow 325° oven until the vegetables are tender, about 1/2 hour. Sprinkle with paprika, and open an alley to the table.

WILD GOOSE LIVERS IN SHERRY

Saute the livers, say about 1/2 pound of them, rapidly in preferably goose grease but otherwise in a tablespoon of butter or margarine, for 5 minutes or until they are soft. Add an equal volume of eggs that have been hard boiled by being simmered, completely immersed in the bubbling water, for 15 minutes. Mix to a paste along with a small minced onion. Season to taste with salt and freshly ground black pepper.

Add 3 tablespoons dry sherry and bring to a boil, then stir in a tablespoon of lemon juice and an additional tablespoon of either goose fat or butter or margarine.

Remove from the heat without additional cooking. Serve either on crackers or on points of thin hot toast. These will put a smell of good cooking in the air.

ROAST RAIL

These rather hen-shaped marsh birds live on a diet of insects, seeds, buds, frogs, mollusks, crustaceans, and aquatic plants, and so, carefully plucked instead of being skinned as is too often done, can be delicious. I like them rubbed inside and out with butter or margarine and with proportionately 1 teaspoon of garlic salt to 1/8 teaspoon of freshly ground black pepper.

Fill with a stuffing made by sauteing until tender 1/2 cup chopped onion and 1/4 cup chopped celery, then combining 1/2 cup cooked wild or brown rice. Wrap birds with strips of salt pork.

Roast half an hour or until tender in a hot 400° oven, basting frequently with the drippings and with melted butter or margarine. Serve with steaming hot bannock—broken, not cut, into individual proportions and dripping with butter. All this is best for an intimate dinner when you're in such a mood that you detest noise and hubbub and sitting among strangers.

FRIED RAIL

Disjoint 2 1/2 to 3 pounds of rail and dip the pieces in milk, saving the remaining milk for the gravy. Season with salt and freshly ground black pepper, mixed proportionately 1 teaspoon of the former to 1/8 teaspoon of the latter. Roll lightly in flour.

Melt 2 tablespoons apiece of butter or margarine, shortening, and bacon drippings or ham fat in a heavy iron frypan over high heat. When the grease has reached a point just short of smoking, put in the pieces of rail, skin sides down. Lower the heat at once and cook slowly, uncovered, until the sections are brown on one side. Then turn, once only, and bronze the fowl on the other side, a process that all in all will take about 1/2 hour. Remove from the skillet and spread on absorbent paper in a warm place.

Drain off any excess grease until there is just enough to cover the bottom of the frypan. Add 2 tablespoons flour mixed to a paste with a little cold water, 1/2 teaspoon salt, 1/8 teaspoon freshly ground black pepper, and 1/8 teaspoon paprika, stirring until everything is smoothly blended. Add 1 cup of milk and another cup of water, pouring these in very slowly and stirring all the while. Once the liquid has all been added, adjust the seasoning by the taste. Simmer over low heat for a dozen minutes. If the gravy becomes too thick during this time, add a bit more milk and water and continue cooking.

Such fried rail, served on a hot platter drenched with the gravy, is something to share, like joy.

MUD HEN, ETC.

Are men the best cooks? The Hudson's Bay Company, drawing on over 300 years of North American experience, says so. In its cooking course aimed at the bachelor managers among its some 200 far-flung fur trading posts, the *Governor and Company of Adventurers of England Trading Into Hudson's Bay* state unequivocally, "The best cooks in the world are men."

My wife Vena suspects that this statement may be inserted largely as a morale builder, because a few sentences further along the potential "world's best chef" is cautioned not to use his dishcloth to wipe off the stove. Yet the majority of good cooks in the Far North, certainly, are male. Some visiting sportsmen never do recover completely from the spectacle of hairy-armed sourdoughs lounging around a fur press and swapping recipes.

These old-timers go in mostly for plain cooking, although occasionally you'll meet a bannock-puncher with a flair for the exceptional. One of these was rotund Ted Boynton, famous for more than a quarter century as one of the best trail cooks in the continental Northwest.

Whenever I see someone discarding some less favored waterfowl because they're "too fishy" or "too gamy" I remember how Ted Boynton used to handle birds of this sort. It's too bad, for several reasons, that more hunters don't know about it. Anyway, I guess one party figured they had Ted stopped the day they lugged in a brace of mud hen. One dude allowed as how he'd tried mud hen before. He said that if the part he got went over the fence last, someone must have given it a boost.

Maybe it was the odors sifting into the atmosphere from the direction of Ted Boynton's fire. Maybe it was just curiosity, for a mud hen, although kind to its family and all, is generally about as tender and tasty as a discarded moccasin. At any rate, there was no second call that evening after the first pan-banging accompanied, "Come and get it." There these fowl were, browned and bulging, looking as handsome as canvasback and smelling no less tempting than fat ptarmingan. Someone stuck his fork gingerly into a drumstick,. Moist steaming meat fell invitingly away from the bone. Everyone dug in hungrily.

"Even a loon doesn't cook up too bad," Ted told us, and later proved it, "if a yahoo don't try to gentle it aitch-for-leather. So don't throw mud hens or other such critters away, particularly in times like these. Skin and take out all fat. Then cram with onions. B'il real easy for 3 hours. Then start brand-new with a crumb stuffing. Tuck a mess of sow belly or bacon strips where they'll do the most good. And roast nice and quiet like until a hungry man can't wait no longer."

When Ted had the birds and the fixings, he sauteed the breasts only of fish-eating ducks in a mixture, enough for four such fowl, of 2 cups of port, 3 tablespoons Benedictine, 2 tablespoons Worcestershire sauce, 2 tablespoons tart currant jelly, 1 cup bacon drippings or margarine, and 1/2 cup apiece of sliced fresh mushrooms and green onions. The results were as tasty as if the birds had been of the grain-feeding brethren.

MERGANSER BREASTS

After soaking them in salt water and cider overnight, skin the breasts of the four mergansers or those of similar fish-eating ducks and remove all possible fat which contains the remaining strong flavor. Simmer in salted water for 1/2 hour. Then drain, cover with fresh cold water, and keep bubbling another 30 minutes. Drain once more.

Fork around a large diced onion and a cup of sliced fresh mushrooms in a stick of butter or margarine in a frypan until tender. Then put in the breasts and brown. Add the contents of an 8-ounce can of tomato sauce, a similar amount of water, 2 jiggers of sherry, a jigger of Benedictine, and simmer until a sharp fork will easily penetrate and withdraw from the largest chunk of meat.

The first time you serve this to hungry friends you'll feel beyond yourself, as though you could smile like the greatest maitre d' and cook like the most famous chef.

BRAISED GALLINGULE

This dark cootlike frequenter of cool marshes, equally at home wading among reeds or swimming with its head-pumping motion, can enhance any table if you'll skin it first and remove all fat.

Disjoint and cut into pieces, taking the time to use a meat saw where necessary rather than a cleaver, and rub liberally with salt and cayenne before browning in a generous amount of butter, margarine, or preferably bacon drippings. Add a little water to prevent burning and cook over moderately low heat for 1/2 hour, stirring every 10 minutes. Then add an 8-ounce can of tomato sauce, a diced clove of garlic, cover, and cook another 1/2 hour or until tender, continuing to stir occasionally. This has a pleasingly wayward flavor, as illusive as a spark.

GAME BIRD LIVERS IN SHERRY

Game bird livers as a whole are so delicate that they should be cooked and served separately the same day they are secured. Here's a way to use them as appetizers while the rest of the meal is cooking, scenting the kitchen with its tantalizing aromas. The recipe is based on 1/2 pound livers, so regulate it accordingly.

Saute the livers rapidly in 2 teaspoons of butter or margarine for 1 minute a side. Season to taste with salt and freshly ground black pepper. Pour on 1 1/2 tablespoons of sherry and bring to a bubble. Then add 2 teaspoons lemon juice and another teaspoon of butter or margarine. Swirl around until the grease is melted and then remove from the heat. Spread on crisp crackers for the group, and make a mental note not to let any more of these succulent little tidbits go to waste.

SPITTED PHEASANT

There is no need for this to be the dry, tough, stringy, tasteless sacrifice so often offered the dispirited hunter. The trouble is that the cook with the rotisserie too often relies on basting to keep this essentially dry fowl moist and tender. With pheasant this just doesn't work.

Instead, enwrap the bird with a thin layer of pork fat, first rubbing it sparingly, inside and out, with a mixture of proportionately 1 teaspoon salt, 1/4 teaspoon rosemary, and 1/8 teaspoon freshly ground black pepper. Also moisten the inside liberally with cooking oil, butter, or margarine. Add 1/2 sliced onion, 1/4 sliced apple, and fill the remainder of the opening with leafy celery tops.

A yound pheasant will take about an hour of turning a foot above medium-red charcoal. When no one can wait much longer, remove the barding and continue spinning another dozen minutes while the bird bronzes.

POTTED PHEASANT

Even a middle-aged pheasant can be dry and stringy unless cooked most advantageously, while under similar conditions an oldster can become a very tooth-defying article indeed. When you have to make a meal of such a bird, especially when its toughness can't be moderated a bit by hanging, disjoint and saw the fowl into sections and roll each piece in a mixture of 1 cup flour, 1 teaspoon garlic salt, and 1/8 teaspoon freshly ground black pepper.

Melt 2 tablespoons of butter or margarine in a casserole over medium heat and fork the pieces around until they are temptingly brown. Then add a large chopped onion and cook until the vegetable just begins to tan. Spoon in two large canned tomatoes, squashing and cutting these into bits. Once everything is seething, add 1 teaspoon salt, 1/2 teaspoon chili powder, and 1/4 cup Metaxa brandy. Then transfer to a slow 325° oven for 2 1/2 hours or until the meat can be easily penetrated by a sharp fork. You'll feel a certain dreamy contentment when sitting down to such a feast.

PHEASANT BREASTS

Sometimes the gunning is so good that you can indulge in a banquet of pheasant breasts, saving the rest of the bird for soup. In a large, heavy, iron frypan melt a stick of butter or margarine and stir in 1/8 teaspoons apiece of thyme, marjoram, chili powder, sage, and minced garlic.

Rub 4 pheasant breasts with, proportionately, 1/4 cup flour, 1 teaspoon salt, 1/2 teaspoon paprika, and 1/2 teaspoon freshly ground black pepper. Brown them in the frypan's bubbling mixture. Then cover and cook over moderate heat until tender.

Place the meat on a prewarmed platter. Add 1/4 cup dry sherry to the juices and bring to a bubble. Pour over the fowl, add sprigs of fresh watercress, and stand out of the way of the rush.

Here's a risotto, friendly as a blazed trail, to go with such a feast. Start things moving, while the pheasant breasts are cooking, by making 3 cups of chicken bouillon by dissolving the necessary cubes or paste in boiling water or, better, by diluting a can of concentrated chicken broth. Add 1/8 teaspoon of saffron and set aside for the moment. Melt 3/4 stick butter or margarine in a large, heavy frypan over low heat and saute 1/2 cup of minced onion, stirring until the bits are pale gold.

Then put in a cup of white rice, 1/4 teaspoon salt, and the broth with the saffron. Stirring continually, cook over low heat until the liquid is absorbed, whereupon the rice should be done. Transfer to a hot platter, scatter on 3/4 cup of grated Parmesan cheese, and serve hot with the fowl. The combination will make the pulses quicken, like the horns in Brahms' piano concerto in B flat major.

BAKED PHEASANT

Divide a pheasant into serving pieces. Rub with proportionately 1/2 cup flour, 1 teaspoon salt, 1 teaspoon paprika, 1/4 teaspoon parsley flakes, and 1/8 teaspoon freshly ground black pepper. Set in a well-oiled roaster, cover liberally with chips of butter or margarine, and

brown in a hot 400° oven for 1/2 hour. Pour in a cup of
boiling water, cover, and bake in a slow 300° oven for 2
hours or until tender. Before bringing to the table, add a
jigger of pale dry amontillado sherry and another of orange
curacao.

PHEASANT IN MUSHROOM SAUCE

Divide a large pheasant into serving pieces. Rub in
proportionately 1 teaspoon garlic salt and 1/8 teaspoon
freshly ground black pepper. Melt 1/2 stick of butter or
margarine in a heavy frypan and brown the meat, turning it
frequently. Then transfer the bird to a casserole.

Add a can of condensed cream of mushroom soup and a
cup of milk to the juices remaining in the frypan and bring
slowly to a bubble, stirring constantly until everything is
smooth and velvety. Pour this sauce over the meat in the
casserole, stir, cover, and bake in a slow 325° oven for 1 1/2
hours or until tender. After an hour, stir in 1/2 cup of your
best dry sherry. The world will seem as bright as a rainbow
reflected in a crystal goblet.

PHEASANT AND SPAGHETTI

Rub your pheasant with butter or margarine and brown
on all sides in a heavy frypan. Then blend 1/2 cup
amontillado sherry, 1/3 cup cooking oil, the juice of 1/2
lemon, 2 tablespoons chopped onion, 1 minced clove garlic,
1/2 teaspoon salt, 1/2 teaspoon freshly ground black
pepper, 1/4 teaspoon thyme, and 1/4 teaspoon marjoram.
Simmer the bird in this sauce, covered, for 1 hour or until
the meat is fork tender.

If you like this as often as we do, you may care to vary it
on occasion, and this is easy to do by adding a large can of
tomatoes. In any event, serve with or over spaghetti. The

combination will make even a difficult day slip gradually back into focus as through hunting binoculars when the eyepieces are being adjusted.

FARMHOUSE PHEASANT

Brush about a 2 1/2 pound pheasant with melted butter or margarine, then brown in a heavy frypan. Finally, cover and simmer 1 hour in a sauce composed of 2 cans of tomato paste diluted half and half with water, 1/4 cup cooking oil, 1/2 bay leaf, 1/4 tablespoon butter or margarine, 1 tablespoon salt, 1/4 teaspoon freshly ground black pepper, 1/4 teaspoon marjoram, and 1/8 teaspoon thyme. The result will be like a silvery air from the seventh century.

PHEASANT PIE

You'll need 2 medium-size pheasants. Put in a large kettle along with a stalk of celery, big onion, clove of garlic, a bay leaf, 2 teaspoons of salt, and 1/2 teaspoon freshly ground black pepper. Cover with water, put on the lid, and cook over low heat for 3 hours or until the meat is falling from the bones. Complete this latter process by hand, discard the skeleton, and strain the broth. Cook a cup of tiny white onions in the broth until they are tender.

Melt 2 sticks of butter or margarine in a pot, then scatter in 1/2 cup flour, stirring until everything is smooth. Then, just as gradually, pour in 2 cups of the broth, stirring all the while. Add a small can of sliced mushrooms, juice and all, and a cup of cream. Simmer, stirring until thickened.

Spread a package of frozen peas across the bottom of a 2-quart casserole. Set the meat, onions, mushrooms, and a small can of sliced pimentos atop them. Pour the sauce and a jigger of brandy over this, reserving at least a 1-inch space at the top.

A good crust for a casserole about 9 inches across can be made by sifting together a cup of sifted flour and 1/2 teaspoon salt. Cut in 1/4 cup shortening. Handling this lightly and quickly, add only enough water—about 3 tablespooons—to make a dough that will stay together when rolled. Roll out and cut to fit, allowing 1/2 inch margin to turn under and press to the casserole with your fork. Prick to prevent puffing, then bake in a hot 450° oven until tan; about 15 minutes. This will be as far away from an ordinary dish as the Peace River is from the equator.

CREAMED PHEASANT

Section a young pheasant and tan sparingly in a stick of butter or margarine. Unless you have a cup of pheasant or chicken broth from another day, prepare a cup of the latter with bouillon or with a diluted 1/2 cup of concentrated chicken broth. Pour over the pheasant and simmer, uncovered, until only several tablespoons of the broth remain.

Add 1 1/2 jiggers of dry sherry and bring again to a bubble. Pour on 2 cups heavy cream, season to taste with salt and freshly ground black pepper, and simmer until thickened. Sprinkle with paprika. Served on hot toast with fresh sprigs of watercress, this will warm an early, cold, clear evening.

PHEASANT JUNIPER

Place a tablespoon of gin or 3 juniper berries inside each of 2 tender young pheasants, truss, lay 2 strips of bacon across the top of each bird as it lies initially breastside up in a heavy skillet, and brown with 1/4 stick of butter or margarine and 1/4 cup of chopped green onions. Then pour 1/4 cup of heated brandy over them and light it.

When the flames ebb away, add 1 1/2 cups pheasant or chicken broth, salt and freshly ground black pepper to taste, dust with paprika, and slide into a preheated hot 425° oven for 1/2 hour. Afterwards, pour 3 cups of heavy cream over the birds, sprinkle with 3 tablespoons freshly grated horseradish, and roast for another 20 minutes or until tender, basting frequently. Serve on a hot platter, drenched with the gravy. This is really something when the last evening sunshine is filtered through the trees, angling like the tight golden strings on some Hindu musical instrument.

BRANDIED PHEASANT

Cut up two pheasants so the meat will cook more evenly. Set on a high rack in a roasting pan, where simmering fluid will not reach it. In the bottom of the pan place 3 large sliced onions, a handful of celery tops, 1 1/2 teaspoons salt, 1/2 teaspoon freshly ground black pepper, 2 jiggers of Metaxa brandy, and enough boiling water to reach within an inch of the rack. Cover tightly and steam in a moderate 350° oven, adding more water as needed.

As soon as the meat is tender, skin and remove from the bones. Take out the rack and place the remaining skin and bones in the steaming water to cook slowly for 3 hours.

In the meantime, spread the preferably large chunks of meat in a bowl, cover with Metaxa brandy, and refrigerate overnight and until ready to use the next day.

Get a medium-size container of wild rice and cook the seeds according to the particular instructions. Using butter or margarine, saute separately in a large heavy frypan 1 large diced onion, 1 cup sliced mushrooms, and 1 cup diced celery. Then mix with the cooked wild rice and 1/2 cup diced roasted chestnuts. In a large casserole, alternate layers of this and the pheasant.

Mix a can of concentrated mushroom soup with an equal amount of the strained stock. Add a jigger of Madeira. Pour the mixture almost to the top of the casserole. Cover and bake in a moderate 325° oven until all but a small amount of the liquid has been absorbed. Sprinkle with paprika, garnish with watercress, and serve hot with orange slices soaked in orange curacao. This will make a meal everyone will recall afterwards with a satisfying vividness.

BAGGED PHEASANT

This novel way of cooking an otherwise rather dry large pheasant does much for its succulency, and it's a cinch to accomplish. Rub the outside of the bird with, proportionately, 1/2 cup flour, 1 teaspoon salt, and 1/8 teaspoon freshly ground black pepper. Sprinkle the inside with fresh lemon juice.

Start your stuffing by dicing 6 slices bacon. Place in a cold frypan, slide over medium heat, and cook until lightly tanned. Then remove the bits and add 1/2 cup diced onion, 1/4 cup diced celery, 2 tablespoons chopped parsley, a mashed garlic clove, and enough diced apples to fill the bird. Cover and cook over the same medium heat until the fruit is tender. Stuff the pheasant loosely with this.

Grease a heavy brown paper bag, place the bird inside, tie the mouth of the bag, and set in a shallow pan in a moderate 375° oven. Check after 1 1/2 hours. Then close to being done if not already right for the table, the skin should be bronzed and crisp, the meat tender and rich.

Place the bird on a serving platter, pour 1/4 cup warmed gin over it, and light this at the table. Everything will be as enticing as an iron balcony in old New Orleans.

PHEASANT VELVET

You'll need about 1/2 pound of cooked pheasant meat for this side dish. Dice the meat, then put it into your blender at low speed, adding from a cup of pheasant or chicken broth—a teaspoon of the liquid at a time—until you have smooth, thin paste. Transfer to a mixing bowl.

Fold in 3 briefly beaten egg whites, the remainder of the cup of broth, 1 tablespoon cornstarch, 1/2 teaspoon salt, 1/2 teaspoon dry sherry, and 1/4 teaspoon monosodium glutamate.

Heat 2 cups of cooking oil over medium heat, to about 300° if you have a cooking thermometer. Spread the pheasant paste into the oil with a tablespoon, immediately adding other layers as soon as the preceding layers are in place. Heat only until the paste is firm, as it should remain white and not allowed to turn brown. Then drain the cooked meat into a colander, saving the oil.

Return 2 tablespoons of the oil to the frypan over moderately high heat. Add a cup of parboiled small peas and 1/4 teaspoon salt, stirring constantly for 1/2 minute. Then add 3/4 cup of pheasant or chicken broth in which 1/2 tablespoon of cornstarch has been well blended, stirring all the while. As soon as the mixture thickens, gently fold in the cooked fowl. Turn out on a prewarmed serving platter, dust with paprika, and enjoy immediately. It'll be as delicate as the sound of stillness, like a breath held in.

PHEASANT PIEDMONTESE

Dust 2 young pheasants with paprika and freshly ground black pepper. Then brown them in a tablespoon apiece of butter or margarine and cooking oil in a Dutch oven, along with 1/8 teaspoon sage, 1/8 teaspoon rosemary, and a crushed bay leaf. When they are well bronzed, remove them for the time being.

Cook 1/2 cup each of diced celery and shredded carrot in the residue in the bottom of the pot. Stir in the contents of a can of condensed onion soup, add 8 small white onions, and replace the pheasants. Simmer over low heat for approximately an hour or until the birds are tender. Then remove them, along with the onions, to a bed of watercress on a hot platter.

Quickly skim the fat off the gravy, then strain the latter. Make a thin paste of 1 1/2 tablespoons sifted flour and 3 tablespoons cold water and stir into the liquid. Simmer, stirring, for 3 minutes and then pour into a gravy boat.

This makes a happy meal when rain has been a diagonal veil all day against the trees, which are now stretching blackly toward the unexpected flush of a cheering sunset.

QUAIL AND WINE

The extra modicum of succulency and flavor afforded by plucking these little birds, then singeing off the more persistent down, is well worth the bother. Then open up along the backbone and remove the entrails, finally wiping the cavity dry with a damp cloth.

Stuff the flavorsome quartet if you want with 1/2 pound chopped fresh mushrooms, 1/3 cup of fine bread crumbs, 1/2 stick of butter or margarine, 1 small diced onion, a teaspoon chopped parsley, 1 teaspoon salt, 1/8 teaspoon freshly ground black pepper, and a minced garlic clove. Truss.

Set in a greased casserole. Add 1 cup golden-colored sauterne and 1 cup cream. Cover and bake in a moderate 325° oven, basting frequently, until tender. Besides being redolent with enticing aromas, these quail will then be as appealing to the eye as the Atlantic Coast's creeping evergreen pixie at the moment its sprawling masses enliven the sandy barrens with star-shaped white flowers.

LATE AUTUMN QUAIL

This is the way I like my quail in the late autumn when they are sweet with the last fruit from the spidery, dead berry bushes. Rub 4 of them inside and out with proportionately a teaspoon salt and 1/8 teaspoon apiece of freshly ground black pepper and fresh paprika. Bronze on all sides over low heat with a stick of butter or margarine in a heavy frypan.

Dust the birds sparingly with 2 tablespoons sifted white flour. Add a can of concentrated chicken broth, 1/2 cup dry sauterne, 1/8 teaspoon thyme, and a bay leaf. Cover snugly so that as little of the flavor will escape as possible and simmer so slowly for 45 minutes, or until the quail are tender, that only the occasional bubble plops to the surface. Serve hot with wild rice, drenched with the juices.

QUAIL IN SHERRY

Open 4 quail along their breasts and press flat. Rub with proportionately 1 teaspoon salt, 1/8 teaspoon freshly ground black pepper, and 1/8 teaspoon paprika, then with softened butter or margarine. Broil 15 minutes or until golden on both sides.

Melt a stick of butter or margarine in a large, heavy frypan, then smoothly stir in 3 tablespoons of flour first mixed into a thin paste with a little water. Then, over low heat, slowly stir in a can of concentrated beef consomme that has been diluted with a cup of warm water, 1/2 cup good sherry, and a blush of cayenne. Once the sauce has bubbled and thickened, spoon in the broiled quail, cover, and simmer 1/4 hour or until the foursome is tender. They'll then be as memorable as onion soup at dawn at Les Halles.

CAMP-STYLE QUAIL

Here's a pleaser, judging from the mail that comes in from my *Gourmet Cooking For Free*, that's simple enough for camp. If, like many of us, you get hungrier than usual when the first chill shiver of autumn crisps the air and the dogs start to stir more restlessly, saute enough onions to go around in a liberal supply of butter or margarine in the frypan, cooking them over low heat until they are tender. Then add the quail, split down the back and flattened.

Cover and simmer until tender, turning at about the halfway point. Season lightly to taste with salt and pepper from a freshly turned mill and serve with the hot sauce. This is really something when trees close to the cabin cast thick, dark shadows over the shakes, and little puffs of breeze rattle through rustling grass, already sere and frostbitten.

QUAIL IN TRENCHERS

Halve 4 quail. Rub proportionately 1 teaspoon salt and 1/8 teaspoon freshly ground black pepper. Heat a stick of butter or margarine in your frypan and saute the birds until they are browned all over. Add 1/2 cup hot water, cover snugly, and steam 1/2 hour or until tender in a moderate 325° oven.

In the meantime, halve 4 fresh rolls, remove their soft centers, place the shells in the oven until toasted, and then brush their crispness with the melted butter and juices remaining in the frypan. Serve each halved quail in a hollowed half-roll on a bed of watercress.

While the cooking is in progress, peel 4 whole pears without removing the stems. Simmer until each is tender to a sharp fork in 1 cup water, 2 tablespoons brown sugar, 1 teaspoon cinnamon, 3 cloves, 1/8 teaspoon salt, and 1/2 teaspoon lemon juice. When done, stir in 1/4 cup brandy. Serve a brandied pear in its proportion of sauce with each 2 trenchers of quail. It'll be as if you have some kind of extra dimension working for you.

QUAIL AND WILD BERRIES

Rub your 4 quail inside and out with salt, freshly ground black pepper, and a little thyme. Then brush with melted butter or margarine, blended with an equal portion of fresh lemon juice.

Cram each bird with freshly picked blueberries, preferably the sweeter, little fellows. Close the opening with toothpick-pinned salt pork.

Fold each bird in heavy-duty foil, leaving a surplus at the top to allow for steam but crimping the edges securely. Roast at a hot 425° for an hour. As with all quail, serve immediately, with the seething juices and hot, buttered, baking powder biscuits. This is a treat, especially when the rolling countryside with its dark spruces and bare

hardwoods, reaching out about you in the silence of approaching winter, is turning blue and hazy.

QUAIL AND GIN

Wrap each of your quartet of quail in salt pork, pinned in position with toothpicks. Saute, turning from side to side, in 2 tablespoons of butter or margarine.

Then transfer to a saucepan, add a cup of boiling water, and 3 ounces of gin. Cover and simmer 1 1/2 hours, adding more water if necessary. Then pour off the liquid and salt and pepper the birds to taste. Tip in 1 1/2 cups of sour cream at this time and simmer for 1/2 hour. If the sour cream should curdle, slowly add a teaspoon of hot water until it smooths again. The results are as intriguing as an Eskimo bear carved from a walrus tusk.

QUAIL AND ALMONDS

Sprinkle 4 quail inside and out with proportionately 1/2 cup flour, 1 teaspoon salt, and 1 teaspoon chili powder. Dice 2 stalks of celery and 1 large onion and saute in 1/2 stick butter. Add a cup of slivered almonds and a diced clove of garlic and mix thoroughly. Season to taste with salt.

Stuff the birds sparingly. Set on breasts in roasting pan, add 1/2 cup of water, and roast in a moderate 325° oven 2 1/2 hours or until the quail are tender.

ADOBE QUAIL

Quail are even easier to cook in the field than in most kitchens. Just roll each bird—feet, head, feathers, and all—in a ball of clay. Place these in the hot ashes by the edge of your glowing hardwood campfire for about 1/2 hour. As soon as the clay is baked into an adobe ball, crack open the shell. With the skin and feathers sticking to it, all will be ready for salt and pepper which, if you've done this before, you'll have in a little waxed-paper wad in your pocket. Quail like this are like time; they'll soon be past, but their memory will remain about you forever.

QUAIL SUPREME

Dredge your quartet of the little birds in a tablespoon of flour and salt and freshly ground black pepper to taste. Using a roaster, heat a stick of butter or margarine and a tablespoon of olive oil just short of smoking. Add the fowl and, turning, brown quickly to seal in the juices.

Lower the temperature, tilt in a cup of boiling water, cover the pan, and cook until tender, adding more water as needed until the moment comes to brown the breasts. Then uncover, simmer the water away, and bronze the birds in the remaining grease.

Once the birds have been removed to a warm platter, stir a tablespoon of flour into the butter and oil. Add 1 cup water and scrape all the brown coating off the roaster into the gravy. Cook until thick, all the time stirring. Pour over the quail and serve. Their taste will be as smooth as a newly opened leaf.

PARTRIDGE IN FOIL

In the old days we used to encase each drawn partridge, its cavity well rubbed with salt and perhaps with a halved clove of garlic, in clay and bury it among the hot coals and ashes of the campfire for half an hour, whereupon it would come out looking like a hot adobe brick. Breaking off the bricklike covering would leave a clean, featherless, skinless, moist, taste-tempting bird.

Now you can do much the same thing with heavy, double-duty aluminum foil, its edges tightly crimped, first rubbing butter or margarine, salt, garlic, and a bit of paprika over the plucked fowl and barding it with thin strips of salt pork. Try substituting a bay leaf for the garlic sometime.

The same foil-wrapped ritual can be accomplished in a pan in a very hot 500° oven at home, although to my taste at least it required about 20% longer cooking time.

SUBARCTIC PARTRIDGE

One thing I'll never forget is the 2 partridge I roasted, then ate by myself on a frost-spangled winter day in the subarctic where, with the temperature hovering a frigid 80° below freezing, I was alone with our frisky wolfhound in our Peace River log cabin, Vena's having ridden out with the mail to Fort St. John for some reason or other.

The 2 birds were large and tough, but I had nothing much to do all day but keep the lodgepole pine fire in the big cook stove crackling while outside the frosted windows trees and river ice cannonaded as they froze even more deeply. I sat close to the blaze with my Alexandre Dumas book, the *Vicomte De Braggelone*, that a few days before I'd found in a deserted prospector's cabin on now-submerged Brennan's Flat, and there was always a pleasant surge of warmth when I opened the oven door to baste the fowl.

What I wanted, I decided, was a moist stuffing so that

the birds wouldn't toughen even more, so from what I had at hand I mixed equal quantities of cream cheese with well-soaked dried apples, then stirred in a minced clove of garlic and 4 tablespoons of rendered black bear fat. Butter or margarine, I proved later, would have served nearly as well.

The brace of spruce hens, amply rubbed with fat and festooned with bacon, each went into a bread pan and into the seething oven. There I basted them with their own juices about every half-hour until the meat was falling away from the bones, by which time the savor of the dressing had delectably diffused through it. At dinner time, when it was dark enough to add the light of my Coleman lantern to the dwindling radiance of the western sky, I made myself fresh bannock atop the stove, broke off steaming chunks that I dipped into the succulent juices, and ate every morsel.

SAUTEED PARTRIDGE BREASTS

When the shooting is good, treat yourself and your guests to this sumptuous repast. You'll need 4 partridge breasts, skinned and then sliced thinly. Immerse each slice into a mixture made of 2 cups sifted flour, 2 teaspoons garlic salt, 1 teaspoon parsley flakes, and 1/2 teaspoon freshly ground black pepper.

In the meantime, be heating a heavy iron frypan. Melt a stick of butter or margarine in this and gently saute the slices, about a dozen minutes a side, until they are crisp and golden.

Way I like these is with broken-off chunks of steaming bannock, dripping with butter, and plenty of hot black tea. In fact, you can take the makings in a plastic bag and prepare this feast on the trail from birds shot on the spot, cooking the slices on forked green sticks and the bannock folded around a heavy green stick and leaned over hot coals.

PARTRIDGE AND FRUIT

When you have an ample dinner built around them, 2 plump partridges will satisfy four diners. When the fowl is to be the main part of the meal, it'll take a bird apiece.

Rub the insides of each fowl with, proportionately, 1 teaspoon salt, 1/4 teaspoon paprika, and 1/8 teaspoon freshly ground black pepper. Stuff each with 4 halved dry apricots, 4 halved dry prunes, and 1/2 a sectioned orange. Brush the exteriors with melted butter or margarine and sprinkle with the same sort of paprika, salt, and pepper mixture.

Set breasts up on a rectangle of heavy-duty aluminum foil apiece, wrap, and crimp. Place in a low roasting pan, breasts still upward, and bake in a slow 325° oven for 2 hours or until tender. Finally, open the foil at the top, brush the breasts with soft butter or margarine, and return to the oven to bronze for 15 minutes. A jugger of brandy over each bird will add to the aroma as you're carrying them expectantly to the table.

Served, with the juices, over steaming white mounds of mashed potatoes, these would stimulate even hypochondriacs.

PARTRIDGE BREASTS WITH MUSHROOMS

Cut 4 cooked partridge breasts into thin slices. Mix with 1 teaspoon dry sherry, 1 teaspoon salt, 1 teaspoon corn starch, 1/2 teaspoon powdered ginger, and 1/4 teaspoon monosodium glutamate.

Drain a 4-ounce can of sliced mushrooms, saving the liquid. Mix this latter with another teaspoon of corn starch and 1/2 teaspoon salt.

Warm a frypan over medium high heat along with 1/4 cup cooking oil. Add the meat mixture and stir for 2 minutes. Then drain the meat into a strainer over a bowl.

Return the oil and juices to the frypan over medium heat. Add the drained mushrooms and stir 1/2 minute. Then add 1/4 cup of strained parboiled green peas, stirring constantly until they are heated. Blend in the well-mixed corn starch and the meat.

As soon as the liquid thickens, serve at once, garnished if you want with 1/4 cup roasted almonds. The moment will seem tall.

GROUSE AND WILD APPLES

Although you want 4 firm, tart apples, not just any wild apples will do, and you may have to rely on a store. But as an early expert on the matter, Henry Thoreau, noted, "Who knows but this chance wild fruit, planted by a cow or a bird on some remote and rocky hillside, may be the choicest of its kind. It was thus the Porter and the Baldwin grow. Every wild apple shrub excites our expectation thus, somewhat as every wild child it is, perhaps, a prince in disguise."

In any event, grouse and wild apples go well together outdoors as well as on the table. Peel, core, and cut the latter into wedges. To go with them you'll need a quartet of small, young grouse, weighing about a pound apiece.

Rub the birds inside and out with proportionately 1 teaspoon salt, 1/8 teaspoon freshly ground black pepper, and 1/8 teaspoon paprika. Bronze them temptingly in a heavy Dutch oven with a stick of butter or margarine and 3 tablespoons cooking oil. Then cut back on the heat, clamp on a lid, and allow to bubble for 3/4 hour or until the grouse are tender.

Warm 1/2 cup of good apple brandy, pour it into the Dutch oven, and touch off with a match. When the blue flames ebb, stir in a can of condensed chicken broth. Keep warm while you saute the sliced wild apple in a frypan with

1/2 stick of butter or margarine until a sharp fork can be easily inserted, then withdrawn, from the still solid fruit.

The Iroquois, although apples which now grow wild in every state were not brought to Massachusetts and the New World until some nine years after the arrival of the Pilgrims, learned to blend maple sugar deliciously with the fruit. This is the thing to do now, although you can substitute 1/4 cup brown sugar with a teaspoon of lemon juice to lend it character.

Pour the steaming sauce into a hot platter. Set the grouse atop it. Surround with the chunks of wild apple. Such a repast is really something during the latter part of the shooting season when the autumn nights are folding quietly one into another.

BLUE GROUSE WITH ALMONDS

Brush a brace of large, carefully plucked plump birds with melted butter or margarine. Sprinkle inside and out with proportionately 1 teaspoon salt, 1/4 teaspoon paprika, and 1/8 teaspoon freshly ground black pepper. Place a tablespoon of orange curacao and a teaspoon of lemon juice in each fowl. Roast in a preheated hot 425° oven 1/2 hour or until tender, brushing frequently with melted butter or margarine and lemon juice. Then move the grouse to a warm platter.

For the sauce, pour 3/4 cup hot water into the roasting pan and, scraping, bring to a simmer. Add this to a frypan in which 1/3 cup sliced almonds have been gently tanning in butter or margarine. Season to taste, add a tablespoon each chopped sugared orange peel and sherry, and tip over the grouse. Garnish with sprigs of fresh watercress. Serve with highbush cranberry jelly if you can come by any, sliced green beans, and buttered bread placed under the broiler and toasted only on that side. Exquisite!

CORNED GROUSE

Cut two grouse into serving portions and marinate 4 hours, turning every 1/2 hour if possible, in a cup of sherry, a minced clove of garlic, 2 teaspoons salt, 1 teaspoon paprika, 1 teaspoon curry powder, 1/4 teaspoon freshly ground black pepper, and 1/8 teaspoon thyme.

Then roll in yellow cornmeal and cook preferably over smouldering charcoal, or under an electric broiler, for 10 minutes a side or until tender. The results will be as spritely as a madrigal.

CREAMED GROUSE

For a really delicious repast, cut 2 grouse into serving portions. Rub these in a mixture of 4 tablespoons flour, 2 teaspoons salt, and 1/4 teaspoon freshly ground black pepper. Then melt a stick of butter or margarine in a large, heavy frypan and, turning the pieces frequently, brown them.

Dust the grouse with a teaspoon of thyme. Pour in a pint of heavy cream and if necessary enough water to cover. Put on the lid and simmer until tender, stirring frequently. Check the seasoning. Then dust with paprika and parsley flakes. Serve with buttered, hot baking powder biscuits. There's rapture to this.

SPITTED PIGEON

The modern city pigeon is a descendant of the rock pigeon that in the Old World dwelled among the cliffs and crevices above the caves in which early man built his first fires. He has been with us since our emergence from the ice ages and has adapted as readily as ourselves to the artificial canyons of man's first walled towns. He has known the Grecian palaces and the metropolises of Byzantium. His cold flat feet, adapted to high and precarious walking, have sauntered in the temples of vanished gods as readily as in Boston's old North Station.

Because today he is just as worthy as ever an occasional part of man's diet, catch a note from the past and spit 4 to 8 pigeons, depending on size and appetites, that have been well rubbed with seasoned salt. Put on the rotisserie over the heat of, preferably, glowing hickory chips.

Mix together a stick of melted butter or margarine, 1/2 cup catsup, the juice of a medium-size lemon, 1 finely minced medium-size onion, 1 crushed clove of garlic, 1 teaspoon tarragon, 1 teaspoon salt, and 1/8 teaspoon apiece of freshly ground black pepper, thyme, Worcestershire sauce, and prepared mustard. Heat along with the birds. Brush liberally over the pigeons 5 minutes before removing them from the fire.

STEWED DOVE OR PIGEON

The habit is to consider the smaller members of the family *Columbidae* as doves and the larger members as pigeons. Both are plump, fast-flying birds with shapely small heads and low cooing calls. Two types live on this continent; the smaller, tannish variety with pointed or rounded tails, such as the mourning dove, and those with fanlike tails such as the domestic pigeon. The sexes look alike. Unless the fowl are especially small, one to each diner will do.

The meat of both species is dark and delicious, varying considerably in relation to the quantity and quality of their diet which ranges from seeds, fruits, waste grain, and insects. Throughout the world there are nearly 300 varieties, so you have plenty of choice.

Pigeons especially have a tendency toward toughness, so it is sound practice to simmer them, in a tightly covered receptacle, in a small amount of some fluid such as salted water or tomato juice either in a slow 300° oven or atop the stove for 1/2 to 3/4 hour or until just tender. In fact, unless your birds are young and reasonably fat, this is good operational procedure with both breeds.

Or set a quartet of these tidbits in a casserole along with 1/2 stick butter or margarine, a diced onion, and a minced clove of garlic and brown. Then add a teaspoon salt, 1/2 teaspoon sage, 1/4 teaspoon cloves, 1/8 teaspoon freshly ground black pepper, 2 tablespoons grated lemon peel, and a quart of sauterne. Cover and simmer in a moderate 325° oven for 3/4 hour or until tender. Thicken the sauce with a little butter and flour that have first been kneaded together. Serve steaming hot. The mind has had its feast. Now comes the palate's turn.

DOVE OR PIGEON CASSEROLE

Cut 4 doves or pigeons into serving pieces and brown in olive or cooking oil. Then tip everything into a baking pan. Add 1/8 teaspoon tabasco sauce and salt and freshly ground black pepper to taste. Garnish with the seeded slices of 2 large oranges and 1 medium-size lemon.

Add the contents of a large can of mushrooms that have been cooked in butter and a cup of chicken bouillon or stock. Cover tightly and set in a preheated slow 300° oven. Basting occasionally, bake for an hour or until tender. When you first smell this cooking you'll be silent for a second, listening to the little sputterings.

ROAST DOVE OR PIGEON

Make some herb salt by thoroughly mixing 1 teaspoon salt, 1/5 teaspoon oregano, 1/5 teaspoon monosodium glutamate, and 1/8 teaspoon freshly ground black pepper. If you are using oregano leaves, first crush them to a powder with a rolling pin on a sheet of waxed paper. Then rub the entire mixture into the 4 birds. Dredge in flour and roast in an open pan with a stick of butter or margarine in a hot 400° oven until bronzed, basting frequently.

Lower the heat to a moderate 325°, add 1/2 cup dry sherry, and roast, still uncovered, for 50 to 60 minutes or until tender, basting every 10 minutes with the juices. Festoon with watercress and serve. Such fowl will grace rather than dominate a table, be it hand-hewn pine or modern teak.

PIGEON OR DOVE PILAF

Roast 4 birds until tender, on a rotisserie preferably, basting them frequently with a marinade made by mixing 1/2 cup Teriyaki sauce, 1/2 cup olive or other cooking oil, and 1/2 cup sauterne. The results will smell and taste so delicious that the first time around you may never get any further.

But for pilaf, remove the meat from the bones. In the meantime, be making 2 cups of broth from the heart, sliced gizzard, and neck.

Now start the actual pilaf by sauteing until tender, covered in a large frypan, a medium-size diced onion, 2 sliced stalks of celery, and 1/2 diced green pepper in 2 tablespoons cooking oil. Add 6 sliced medium-size mushrooms, 2 cups of the giblet and neck broth augmented with chicken bouillon powder and hot water if this is necessary to bring the liquid to the desired amount, and warm the mixture to the boiling point.

Then stir and smooth in 2 cups of Minute Rice, cover tightly, and let stand over low heat 5 minutes. Mix in 3 tablespoons grated Parmesan cheese and 1 tablespoon soy sauce and serve steaming hot. It'll be like honey and velvet.

DOVES AND BANNOCK

Rub 4 doves with proportionately 1 teaspoon salt, 1/8 teaspoon freshly ground black pepper, and 1/8 teaspoon paprika. Flour generously. Then brown in margarine or butter, turning the birds so that they will color evenly.

Remove the doves to a hot platter for the moment and shift the skillet to lower heat. Thicken the juices with beurre manié, made by kneading 4 tablespoons of butter with 6 tablespoons flour until you attain a smooth paste. With a wire whip, beat this into the hot liquid, then return to the low heat. Stirring constantly, bring the sauce to a simmer for a minute or 2, until the mixture is thick enough to coat a spoon. At this point return the doves, cover, and cook slowly until tender.

Have bannock baking in the oven, ready to come out when the birds are done. If you've never made this frying pan bread before, mix 4 cups all-purpose flour, 4 teaspoons double-action baking powder, and 1 teaspoon salt. Cut in 3/4 cup of butter or margarine with 2 knives, or with a pastry blender, until the mixture resembles coarse meal.

When everything is ready to do, quickly stir in, little by little, about 1 1/3 cups of cold milk until you have a soft, light, non-sticky dough. Put in a greased pan and bake 12 to 15 minutes in a very hot 450° oven, until an inserted toothpick comes out clean. Break into 4 slabs, place on hot plates, and serve a dove and gravy on each. This is as old-fashioned a delight as the crunch of surry wheels, the creak of harness, and the clip-clop of sweating horses.

DOVES AND WILD RICE CROQUETTES

Season 4 doves with salt and freshly ground black pepper to taste and place in an open roasting pan, along with 3 tablespoons vegetable oil, in a hot 400° oven until they brown, basting frequently.

Add 1 medium-size diced onion, 1 medium-size carrot, 1 stalk sliced celery, and a clove of diced garlic. Let simmer in a moderate 325° oven for about an hour or until the meat is tender.

Blend 2 sticks of butter or margarine with 1 cup sifted flour and cook slowly over very low heat, stirring constantly to achieve a perfect wedding of the 2 ingredients. Continue this until the roux is golden brown.

In the meantime, be cooking 1/2 pound of wild rice in 2 cups giblet broth or chicken bouillon for some 50 minutes or until fluffy. Then add 3 tablespoons white bread crumbs, 1 beaten egg, 5 tablespoons melted butter or margarine, salt and freshly ground black pepper to taste, and mix until pasty. Roll into small balls.

Rotate these balls in 2 tablespoons flour, dip into a whipped egg, and then roll in 1/4 cup of white bread crumbs. Get a pot of deep fat seething at 400°, spoon in the balls, and let cook 2 1/2 minutes or until golden.

Place the birds and vegetables on a hot platter. Surround with the wild rice croquettes. Pour the hot roux over everything, and get out of the way.

ROAST WOODCOCK

Except for an occasional change of pace the taste of woodcock, which are perhaps the most delectable of the game birds, should not be impinged upon by strong outside flavors. Roast woodcock is a case in point. Split the tiny fowl lengthways and flatten each by smacking it smartly with a heavy knife or cleaver. Rub with olive oil and with proportionately 1 teaspoon salt and 1/8 teaspoon freshly ground black pepper, plus a scattering of paprika. Figure on certainly no less than one bird per diner, more ideally two.

Place bony side down in an open roaster with a stick of butter or margarine. Roast in a very hot 450° oven for 5 minutes. Then lower the heat to a moderate 325° and continue cooking 25 minutes or until tender, briefly opening the door and spooning the golden liquid over them every 5 minutes.

DEEP-FRIED WOODCOCK

The dark meat of the evasive, little, long-billed woodcock is so flavorsome that, with each diner thus self-compelled to clean up every last tidbit, one will do for each feaster although two apiece will be better.

When you have brought enough for all back to camp, dry-pluck each without drawing it. Rub with salt, freshly ground black pepper, and a whisper of tarragon. Then lower into a pot of deep oil that is being kept heated to about 365°.

Once the birds have danced for half a dozen minutes, the entrails will have compacted into a clean hard ball that can be discarded, along with the bones, while the perfectly cooked meat is relished to the fullest.

ROASTED WOODCOCK OR SNIPE

The little birds are similar in appearance and habits. Carefully dry-pluck, clean, and draw, doing this latter through a small slit above the vent. The tiny liver and heart may then be returned to the cavity, which should be skewered shut.

Rub the miniature fowl well with butter or margarine, salt, freshly ground black pepper, and a whisper of thyme. Cross the breasts with thin slices of salt pork. Put on a rack in a low pan and roast in a hot 400° oven about 25 minutes or until done, brushing every 5 minutes with melted butter. Results are almost sinfully superb.

For the gravy, stir enough flour, previously mixed to a thin paste with double its volume of cold water, with the juices over low heat until it bubbles to a rich deliciousness.

BROILED SNIPE OR WOODCOCK

Some natives esteem the stomach contents of such animals as the caribou, for such greens, mixed as they are with the digestive acids, are not unlike salad prepared with vinegar. Also, as I pointed out in *Living Off The Country*, other aborigines do not bother to open the smaller birds and animals they secure but pound them to a pulp which is tossed in its entirety into the pot.

Likewise, many gourmets prefer such upland birds as snipe and woodcock cooked with the intestines left inside. These entrails are afterwards removed, chopped mixed with butter and perhaps wine or brandy, and spread on toast.

If you want to try broiled snipe or woodcock this way, pluck the little birds but do not draw or even open them. Rub them well with butter or margarine, salt, and a little freshly ground black pepper. Broil them not too close to the heat for about 25 minutes, turning them frequently so as to cook them evenly. Season to taste. Serve on crisp buttered toast with or without the chopped innards.

BAKED WOODCOCK OR SNIPE

Dry-pluck and draw the birds, then rub with butter or margarine, salt, freshly ground black pepper, and a breath of allspice. Bronze in olive oil or other cooking oil in a frypan. Then move to a casserole and pour a couple of tablespoons of either sweet or sour cream over each. Bake in a moderate 375° oven for about 25 minutes or until tender. Spoon the hot juices over the sputtering fowl. The result is like an intriguing foreign voice, with only the most pleasant trace of an accent.

TAMING A WILD TURKEY

This crown prince of the game birds, one of the rightfully most valued of all trophies, has a delectable wild flavor that elevates it far above the customary holiday fowl. Because of feeding routines, you do not find this savor in the so-called wild turkey from game farms. Actual wild turkey, though, because of these same living and dining habits, are leaner and tougher than their domesticated counterparts, and you have to take this into account in taming them for the table.

You can do this even without an oven, a boon if you're in camp or if you'd like to center the festivities around the patio. Disjoint and saw the fowl into serving portions. Rub the tidbits with salt and with a very generous amount of butter or margarine. Set on a large, double rectangle of heavy-duty aluminum foil and wrap, staunchly crimping all edges. Place in a moderate 325° oven, on a grill over glowing charcoal, or in the hot ashes at the edge of a small hardwood campfire that has burned to coals.

Cook 1 1/2 hours, gingerly turning the packet every 15 minutes to assure even cooking and basting. When the crowning moment of unwrapping arrives, be careful not to let any of the juices escape. Distribute them in cups so that each banqueter can punctuate his forkfuls of steaming meat by immersing them in the seething savoriness. I'll never forget first eating such wild turkey on a hillside California patio, below which the Coast highway cut a deep swath through the ranches, proclaiming its presence by a parade of headbeams which glowed and wavered as they streamed along the Pacific.

ROAST WILD TURKEY

Speed the cooling of the meat by opening and drawing this giant of the game birds as soon as possible after bagging it. Then, taking as much care as feasible to avoid tearing the skin, pluck. Singe off the remaining down. Sever the neck close to the shoulder and disjoint the legs just below the plump drumsticks. If as may be the case you wish to cook part of the bird for Thanksgiving and the rest for Christmas, cut in half along the center of the breast and relegate the more intact portion to the freezer.

Let's say you're roasting the whole bird at once and want also to enjoy some sumptious stuffing. Place the heart, neck, and the cleaned gizzard in a saucepan with a quartered onion, 2 quartered cloves of garlic, 2 sliced celery stalks, 1 tablespoon chopped parsley, and 1 teaspoon salt. Cover with water, bring to a boil, and then reduce the heat and simmer until the gizzard is tender.

Bone the neck and chop the meat with the giblets. For a 15-pound fowl, mix 8 cups crumbled corn bread, the strained giblets, 2 eggs whipped in 2 tablespoons rum, 1 teaspoon poultry seasoning, and salt to taste. Add enough of the strained giblet juices to moisten, along with 1/2 stick melted butter or margarine, and blend well. Stand the turkey on what remains of its neck and lightly drop the stuffing in by the spoonful, being sure not to pack it. Then sew the opening so that the stuffing will remain delightfully dry. Skewer the neck skin. Truss the bird.

Set the turkey on its back atop a rack in a shallow pan. Brush with melted butter or margarine, repeating every 1/2 hour for the next 3 hours. After this the wild bird should be covered with a dripping-moistened cloth to keep it from drying and browning further. Roast for about 4 1/2 hours or until the thigh bone moves easily and a sharp fork can be readily inserted into a leg. Then transfer to a hot platter and let stand a dozen minutes before serving. Try this sometime when a holiday moon hangs clear and silvery lemon in the heavens, and wind-lulled waves break like tinkling crystal on the beach.

SLICED WILD TURKEY AND HAM

When you have a big wild bird to eat your way through, here's the way to enliven a lunch. Cut off 4 generous slices of the white breast meat. Melt 4 tablespoons butter or margarine in a pan and brown the slabs with a diced 1/2 medium-size onion, and a diced clove of garlic.

Then add a cup of dry sherry and 2 jiggers brandy. Bring to a bubble, set afire with a match, and shake the pan until the flames burn themselves out. Simmer off about 1/2 the remaining liquid. Fork out the turkey.

Beat 2 egg yolks into a cup of heavy cream and add this to the sauce. Cook until thick, all the time agitating with a fork to prevent lumping.

Lay a hot slice of sourdough toast on each of 4 warmed plates, spread a slice of boiled ham atop each, then a slab of turkey, and pour the strained sauce over everything. Serve hot. You'll savor the somehow acrid-sweet autumn flavor.

PRAIRIE CHICKEN AND SHERRY

Brown the breasts and thighs of 2 prairie chickens in 1/2 stick of butter or margarine, 1 teaspoon salt, and 1/8 teaspoon freshly ground black pepper. When slightly golden, add 1/2 cup of your best sherry, cover immediately, simmer 1/2 hour or until tender, and serve over steaming rice. This method is satisfyingly simple and memorably exotic.

FAR EASTERN PRAIRIE CHICKEN

Skin 2 prairie chickens and disengage the thighs and breasts. Immerse them one by one in 1/2 cup of any sauce. While they are still moist but not dripping, rub with 1/2 cup flour, 2 tablespoons powdered ginger, and 1 tablespoon paprika.

Saute over low heat in a heavy frypan with 1/2 stick butter or margarine until tan and tender. Salt and pepper to taste and serve. This makes for an amiable repast.

ROAST PRAIRIE CHICKEN

Pluck and singe your large prairie chicken. Rub the inside with 1/2 lemon.

Stuff with 2 cups stale bread crumbs, 1/2 stick melted butter or margarine, 1 small chopped onion, 1 stalk chopped celery, 1 teaspoon salt, 1 teaspoon paprika, 1 teaspoon marjoram, 1/4 teaspoon thyme, and 1/8 teaspoon freshly ground black pepper. Sew or skewer the opening. Rub butter or margarine over the outside of the bird and dust with salt and a few parsley flakes.

Wrap in heavy-duty aluminum foil, leaving room for expansion and crimping the edges tightly. Roast in a moderate 325° oven for 2 hours or until tender, opening the foil the last 15 minutes for browning. There's a flamboyance to this, devious in its pleasant mingling of aromas.

ROAST PTARMIGAN

Rub 4 plucked ptarmigan inside and out with proportionately 1 teaspoon salt and 1/8 teaspoon freshly ground black pepper. Prepare stuffing with 4 cups of dry bread crumbs, 2 medium-size diced onions, 1 minced clove of garlic, 2 teaspoons salt, 1 teaspoon sage, 1/2 teaspoon pepper, and a stick of butter or margarine. Fill cavities and leave open.

Crisscross each bird with 4 strips of bacon and arrange on their backs on a rack in a roasting pan. Tip 1/2 cup boiling water into the pan and roast in a very hot 450° oven for 15 minutes, then reducing the heat to a moderate 325° and cooking 1/2 hour longer or until the tidbits are tender. The last dozen minutes take off the bacon, brush with melted butter or margarine, and brown. On the serving platter, pour 2 jiggers of warmed gin over the birds and ignite it. I'll never forget the first night I did this, for outside the hills were blazing with lightning like a silver fresco.

PTARMIGAN AND DUMPLINGS

Divide 2 large ptarmigan into serving portions. Dredge in flour, seasoned with proportionately 1 teaspoon salt and 1/8 teaspoon freshly ground black pepper, and brown in a frypan with 1/2 stick butter or margarine and 2 tablespoons olive oil.

Then place in a large pot along with a diced onion, 1/2 cup diced carrots, 1/2 cup green peas, and salt and freshly ground black pepper to taste. Cover with cold water, bring slowly to a bubble, cover, and simmer for 2 1/2 hours or until tender.

About a dozen minutes before the meal bring the liquid to a boil. Sift together 1 1/2 cups pastry flour, 1 1/2 teaspoons double-action baking powder, and 3/4 teaspoon salt. Work 1 tablespoon butter or margarine into the dry mixture. When everything is ready to go, make a dent in the middle of the flour mixture, pour in 3/4 cup milk, and fold together very rapidly.

Drop by the rounded tablespoon, not too close together, atop the seething broth in a single layer and cover immediately. Wait 2 minutes, then remove the lid long enough to turn each dumpling once with a quick, deft hand, never letting the boiling cease. Cook some 7 minutes more or until the dumplings are light and fluffy. Then remove the dumplings to a hot plate and thicken the liquid with 2 tablespoons of flour. Serve at once. This is a heartening dish when, outside, hail comes hurrying over the pine tops with a marching sound.

PTARMIGAN PIE

Place 2 plump ptarmigan in a large pot along with 1/2 pound salt pork plus salt and freshly ground black pepper to taste, cover with water, put on the lid, and simmer until tender. Bone the birds. Then simmer the broth, uncovered, until it is reduced by about 1/2 and is rich and strong.

Melt 2 tablespoons of butter or margarine in a saucepan, gradually stir in 2 tablespoons flour, and cook until crumbly. Stirring constantly, pour in the broth and simmer uncovered until it thickens, then season to taste with freshly ground pepper, salt and paprika.

Sift together 2 cups flour, 1 1/2 tablespoons double-action baking powder, and 1/4 teaspoon salt. Work 2 tablespoons butter or margarine and 2 tablespoons shortening into the dry ingredients. Make a depression in the middle and pour in 2/3 cup of real churned buttermilk. Knead just enough, on a floured board or piece of plastic, to form a dough.

Roll 1 1/2 inches thick and line a greased baking dish, putting the remainder of the dough into the refrigerator. Fill with the ptarmigan and gravy and bake in a hot 400° oven. Then roll out the remaining dough to fit the top of the baking dish and bake separately in a preheated 400° oven until flaky. Set on top of the ptarmigan pie and serve, all hot and crisp. The promise will be no less exciting in actuality than it was in preparation.

PTARMIGAN BREASTS

This is for when the gunning has been good, for you'll need 8 ptarmigan breasts. Arrange in a shallow casserole, add salt and freshly ground black pepper to taste, and pour in a cup of light cream. Then festoon with thin strips of butter or margarine, dust with paprika, and sprinkle with parsley flakes. Bake in a slow 325° oven for 25 minutes or until the birds are fork tender. They'll then be no less overmastering than a sunset on the redland buttes of New Mexico.

CHOICE CHUKAR

These game birds, like sandy-hued quail with brilliant red legs and bills, light throats bordered by a clean-cut black necklace, boldly barred sides, and ruddy tails, can be delectable. Dry-pluck them, draw, and cut into serving portions.

Allow 2 chukar to soak an hour in heavy cream, then dredge with flour, and scatter on salt and freshly ground black pepper to taste. Stir around a diced onion until tender in a stick of butter or margarine. Saute the brace of birds in this until they are golden.

Add 1 1/2 cups chicken bouillon, or concentrated chicken broth diluted half and half with water, 1/3 cup fresh lemon juice, 2 tablespoons Worcestershire sauce, and 1 tablespoon orange curacao. Cover snugly and simmer slowly for 45 minutes. Serve on rice, preferably wild, with the pan liquor. Because of the excellence of chukar cooked this way, even the most jaded will forget to be bored.

CROW BREASTS

Tasting like chicken with savory overtones of duck, the dark meat of the crow is well worth bringing home. If you've too many for deep freeze and friends, even when offered to the latter under the more enticing name of rook by which they are retailed in some markets, why not banquet on the breasts?

First rubbing with proportionately 1 teaspoon salt and 1/8 teaspoon freshly ground black pepper, brown the 4 chunks of crow in 1/2 stick of butter or margarine in your skillet, heating the grease just short of smoking, putting in the meat, covering, and cooking covered over moderate heat 7 minutes to a side.

Then add a cup of sherry, put on the lid once more, and simmer until the meat is tender.

Remove the sizzling slabs and arrange atop a 1 1/2-inch layer of steamed wild and brown rice in a flat pan. Add a cup of heavy cream to the juices in the skillet, and stirring, bring to a bubble for a minute. Then remove from the heat and stir in a beaten egg yolk. Pour this sauce over the crow breasts, sprinkle liberally with your favorite kind of grated cheese, and brown under the broiler before serving. They'll then be as satisfying as a refreshing breeze, filigreed with fog moving in from the ocean on a hot afternoon.

chapter three

SMALL GAME

FRESH, PLUMP, RARE meat is the single natural food that includes all the nutritional ingredients necessary for mankind's health. Neither anything else, not any particular parts, need be eaten. Sputtering steaks, if that is what you prefer, will provide all the vitamins, minerals, and other nourishment needed to keep you robust even if you consume nothing else except water for a month, a year, or a decade.

What's one way to help accomplish this to some degree in gourmet fashion during these days of high prices? By not passing up the small game that is freely available to many of us, often throughout the entire year, and which in numerous instances, as when there is a woodchuck or crow shooter in the family, if not eaten will only be wasted.

Much small game is considerably more of a treat than

deer, elk, moose, and their kind because of its fat. For this reason, racoon, opposum, and such should be used within three months when frozen as the fat does not keep well. In contrast, the lean hare or rabbit, with which dietwise you will need added fat in some part of your meal, will retain its fine texture and flavor for up to a year. Otherwise, handle, package, freeze, and store small game according to the general directions suggested in the chapter on big game.

RABBIT AND CHESTNUTS

To preserve all their natural, too often overpowered succulence, roast a brace of young rabbits until fork tender in a low uncovered pan in a slow 325° oven, seasoning them only by brushing with melted butter or the best margarine. Or do the same thing on your rotisserie.

Serve hot with chestnut puree made by boiling 1/2 cup diced celery, the drained contents of 2 11-ounce cans of chestnuts, and a can of condensed chicken broth in an open saucepan until nearly dry. Then pulverize in the blender or by pressing through a sieve. Stir in 1/3 cup of light cream and a tablespoon of butter or margarine. Dust with paprika. This is like sudden late-afternoon sunshine after a long, wet week.

RABBIT A L'ORANGE

Dust about a 3-pound rabbit inside and out with freshly ground black pepper, salt, and paprika before roasting it, with a stick of butter or margarine, in an open shallow pan, in a preheated hot 400° oven for half an hour.

While this is going on, boil a pound of small white onions in water until they are tender. Then drain them, add 2 tablespoons of butter to the saucepan, and glaze them, adding 1/2 teaspoon salt and 1/8 teaspoon of pepper. Put the onions in the rabbit, together with a diced carrot, 1/2 teaspoon thyme, 1/8 teaspoon ground cloves, and a bay leaf. Roast another 15 minutes.

This will give you time to peel 2 navel oranges, grate the peel, cover this with bubbling water, and set to one side until you are ready for it.

Unless you already have some Brown Sauce, make a cupful by dicing an onion and sauteing it in 2 tablespoons bacon fat until both are brown. Then smoothly stir in 2 tablespoons sifted flour that has first been turned into a thin paste with a little water, 1/2 teaspoon salt, 1/8 teaspoon freshly ground black pepper, and a dusting of sugar. Bit by bit, pour in a cup of beef consomme, bring to a bubble, and then cook over very low heat for 10 minutes. Add 1/4 cup of this sauce to the rabbit, saving the rest in the refrigerator to serve sometime over cold meat slices. At the same time pour 1/4 cup of port over the rabbit and continue roasting. Once the meat is tender, fork it onto a hot platter atop a steaming bed of brown rice and keep warm.

Strain the remaining juices from the roasting pan into a saucepan, stir in a can of concentrated chicken broth, and scatter on the drained orange rind. Bring to a bubble, then stir in 2 tablespoons currant jelly.

Alternate the glazed onions around the rabbit with sliced orange, festoon with a few sprigs of watercress, and pour on the sauce. The taste-tingling splendor, and the fragrance, will be like walking suddenly into one of the great restaurants of the world.

BORDER RABBIT

Rabbit we've enjoyed while living on the edge of the desert in New Mexico were enlivened by some of the heat and color of the spice-conscious nation to the south. Two 1-pound rabbits will handily serve four if you'll split each in half. Rub the pieces liberally with salt and garlic, especially the latter, then dredge lightly in flour.

Start the cooking by browning 2 small chili peppers in a Dutch oven with 1/2 cup cooking oil. Then, working over the Dutch oven, crush the peppers through a sieve to extract the juice. Discard the pulp. Brown the meat until golden, forking it around to cover both sides. Then cover and simmer an hour or until fork tender. Spoon away the excess fat.

Toward the end, melt 2 tablespoons of butter or margarine in a separate, good-sized pot. Saute a cup of sliced fresh mushrooms, 1/2 cup diced onion, a large shredded carrot, and 3 tablespoons diced green pepper until soft.

Stir in a tablespoon of flour into a can of concentrated chicken broth, first making a paste of the flour and a tablespoon of the broth and then adding it smoothly to the whole. Pour this gradually into the vegetable mixture over low heat, all the time stirring. Add the juice of a medium-size orange. Stir until bubbles appear and the sauce begins to thicken.

Add 3 tablespoons peanut butter, 2 tablespoons grated orange peel, 1 tablespoon of the small flattish sesame seeds, 1/2 teaspoon aromatic cumin seeds, 4 whole cloves, 1/8 teaspoon nutmeg, and salt and freshly ground black pepper to taste. Simmer about a dozen minutes or until the rabbit in its Dutch oven is ready, stirring every now and then. Skim the fat from the top of this sauce.

Arrange the quartet of halved rabbits on a hot platter and pour the sauce over them. Sprinkle with paprika for an added fillip of vitamins and color. Festoon with chopped watercress and serve. It'll be as if the light slanting on this is from another world.

FRIED RABBIT

The rabbit, North America's most widely hunted game, has such a weak abdominal wall that if it is held up by the front feet for any length of time, its organs will sag and it will die. It follows, therefore, that a bagged rabbit is extraordinarily easy to clean. Just slit from vent to ribs, hold by the forelegs, and give a swift snap. Wipe the cavity with dry grass, remove the head, cut off the feet, and you're finished. The heart and liver can then be salvaged if you want.

Taking off the skin will allow the meat to cool more rapidly, and this peels off as easily as a glove. Just open it up with a cut around the middle at right angles to the backbone so that you can pull a half with each hand. Place each rabbit in a clean paper bag and stow in your packsack or game pocket. They won't be too fresh to enjoy fried that evening, our favorite way of cooking these tidbits. You'll need at least 1/2 pound of meat for each serving, so a large varying hare will handily satisfy four.

Disjointing instead of cleavering whenever possible, cut the rabbit or hare into serving portions. Immerse each piece in milk, then salt and freshly ground black pepper, and finally roll lightly in flour.

Arrange the pieces, meaty sides down, in a frypan over high heat, along with 1/2 stick butter or margarine and 1/4 cup cooking oil. Lower the temperature immediately, cooking uncovered until the pieces are brown on one side. Then turn, once only, and bronze the other side. The meat will be crisp and ready to eat in about 1/2 hour. Lay it out on crumbled absorbent paper where it will keep warm until you can make the gravy.

For this, tilt out all the fat except barely enough to cover the bottom of the frypan. Stir in 2 tablespoons flour, 1/2 teaspoon salt, and 1/8 teaspoon pepper, smoothing it into a paste. Pour a cup of milk, including that in which you dipped the meat, and a cup of water into the frypan, constantly stirring. Keep bubbling over low heat for a dozen minutes, gradually adding more milk and water if the gravy thickens too much. With everything served hot, the gravy has enough discreet character to turn everything into a gourmet's dream.

GYPSY RABBIT

This is so good cold that it will do no harm to make a little extra. Shake 4 pounds of disjointed and cut-up rabbit, several pieces at a time, in a paper bag with 1/4 cup of sifted flour that you've seasoned to taste with freshly ground black pepper, salt, and parsley flakes. During this time have a large, heavy frypan warming over low heat.

Now saute a cup of chopped white onion in 1 1/2 tablespoons of olive or other good cooking oil and an equal amount of either butter or margarine, cooking them only until they are soft but not brown. Then, piling the onions to one side, bronze the rabbit.

Tip in bubbling water to cover, about a quart. Add a cup of raw rice, a teaspoon of seasoned salt, and a teaspoon of paprika. Then clamp on the lid and simmer 20 minutes.

Shift to a well greased 2 1/2-quart casserole, cover, slide into a preheated moderate 325° oven, and bake 1 1/2 hours or until the meat is tender, gingerly lifting off the cover for the last 15 minutes so that most of the juices will be absorbed and the top temptingly tanned. Finally, stir in a cup of sour cream, decorate with a bit more paprika, and serve very hot. Such a dish is a satisfying blend of heartiness and richness, simplicity and sophistication.

RABBIT ASPIC

Simmer a whole, dressed, 3 or 4-pound rabbit until tender throughout, first covering it with cold water. Then fork out the rabbit. While you're boiling the uncovered broth down to 4 cups, bone the meat and cut it into bite-size pieces, working across the grain as much as possible. Then season to taste with salt, freshly ground black pepper, paprika, and parsley flakes.

Add 4 tablespoons (envelopes) of gelatin, soaked in 1/4 cup cold water, to the quart of bubbling stock. Season with a tablespoon Worcestershire sauce and salt to taste. Then add 1/2 cup of chopped stuffed olives and the meat, stirring everything well. Pour into a special mold or bread pan, cool, and finally chill in the refrigerator until it sets. Doled out on crisp lettuce and yellowly topped with cold mayonnaise, there's a joy to this like monarch butterflies dancing in the sunlight.

RABBIT QUEBEC

Cut and disjoint 3 pounds of rabbit pieces, dry with paper toweling, and brown in a frypan with 1/4 stick of sputtering butter or margarine. Then season to taste with salt, freshly ground black pepper, and vitamin-replete paprika. Arrange in a casserole and sprinkle with 1/2 cup of diced onion and a clove of minced garlic.

Stir 2 cups of good dry sherry into the hot juices remaining in the frypan, scrape and mix, then pour over the meat. Cover and bake 2 hours or until tender in a moderate 325° oven. This is relaxing after a day in the hot sun and the resinous smell of spruce.

CREAMED RABBIT

This is so good that four banqueters will be able to do away with 3 pounds of rabbit pieces handily. First rub these with proportionately 1 teaspoon salt, 1/8 teaspoon freshly ground black pepper, and 1/8 teaspoon parsley flakes, then dip lightly into flour. Place in a hot frypan, in which you've melted a stick of butter or margarine, and saute over low heat until golden. Then remove the bits to a warm place.

To the grease and juices remaining in the frypan add a cup of freshly sliced mushrooms and 1/4 cup diced white onion. As soon as the latter is tan and tender, stir in 1/2 cup of good dry sherry and a can of condensed chicken broth. Return the meat, cover, and simmer some 45 minutes or until the rabbit, depending on its size and age, is tender.

Remove the meat to a hot platterful of buttered noodles. Take 1/2 cup of heavy cream. Make a thin paste of a little of this and 3 tablespoons sifted flour. Then mix the paste and the remainder of the cream and stir into the pan juices. Move the receptacle to low heat and, all the time stirring, cook until the contents simmer and thicken. Pour over the rabbit, dust with paprika, and serve. This is just the thing to whet even tiny appetites when the air has the bittersweet, damp, brown scent of fall.

RABBIT AND GIN

Ably prepared rabbit, with its elusive flavor, usually has the delicate suggestion of chicken, but flame it with gin and it takes on the juniper subtlety of the similarly white-meat-ed pheasant.

Brown some 2 pounds of rabbit, cut into serving pieces, in a stick of butter or margarine. Then move to a casserole, pour on 1/2 cup of warmed gin, and light. Once the flames have pronged away, add a cup of chicken bouillon, a small diced onion, and a halved and crushed clove of garlic. Bake in a moderate 350° oven for 1/2 hour, basting about every dozen minutes.

Then add a quart carton of cottage cheese, creamed in the blender, and 2 4-ounce bottles of prepared horseradish. Bake an additional hour or until tender. Scatter on a cup of small, stemmed button mushrooms that have just been sauteed in butter or margarine, dust with paprika, and serve on a bed of rice pilaf.

RABBIT WITH ARTICHOKE

Rub a couple of 2-pound rabbits inside and out with proportionately 1 teaspoon salt and 1/8 teaspoons apiece of freshly ground black pepper and parsley flakes. Roast in a preheated moderate 325° oven for 1 1/2 hours or until tender. Set aside to cool. Then bone, ending up with as large pieces as possible.

Saute a cup of sliced mushrooms, a chopped clove of garlic, and a tablespoon of chopped green onions in 1/4 stick of butter or margarine over low heat until the mushrooms start to wilt. Add a package of frozen artichoke hearts, 1/4 cup dry sherry, and the meat. Cover and bring to a simmer for 15 minutes.

For the sauce, melt 2 tablespoons of butter or margarine in a saucepan. Mix 2 tablespoons of flour into a thin paste with a little water and stir this smoothly into the grease. Add a cup of cream, another 1/2 cup of dry sherry, a tablespoon of Madeira, and 1/8 teaspoon nutmeg, and bring to a bubble. Season to taste with salt and freshly ground black pepper, and simmer another 2 minutes.

Heap the rabbit on a hot platter. Spoon the sauce over it. Garnish with triangles of hot toast, golden with garlic butter. Try this sometime when the full moon is hidden by the clouds that has turned them as silver as an original kopeck.

BRAISED RABBIT TIDBITS

Remove some 1 1/2 pounds of rabbit meat from the bones, cutting the larger chunks into bite-size portions. Roll in flour seasoned to taste with garlic salt, freshly ground black pepper, and paprika. Then begin to brown in a large frypan with 3 tablespoons of preferably olive oil or of some other good vegetable oil.

Before the rabbit is thoroughly golden, add 4 thinly sliced large carrots, 1 thinly sliced large onion, and 1 thinly sliced green pepper. When everything is satisfactorily tan, pour in a large can of tomatoes, cover, and simmer an hour or until the meat is tender. Serve over hot rice. This is really something when over against the dining room windows night has lowered its shadows, mink-colored in the moonlight.

ROAST STUFFED RABBIT

To serve four with this recipe you'll need a couple of tender, 2-pound rabbits. Start the stuffing for these by sauteing a finely chopped, medium-size, white onion, a cup of finely chopped fresh mushrooms, and 2 chopped livers in a couple of tablespoons of butter or margarine for 5 minutes in a small frypan over low heat.

Then move them to a bowl along with 1/2 pound of sausage meat, a tablespoon of chopped parsley, a crushed small clove of garlic, a teaspoon salt, 1/4 teaspoon thyme, and 1/8 teaspoon freshly ground black pepper. Mix thoroughly, then stuff the 2 rabbits with the results, skewering the openings.

Rub the skin liberally with softened butter or margarine, dust with paprika and tarragon, and place the little animals on their backs in a roasting pan with 1/4 cup of good dry sauterne. Cook in a preheated moderate 350° oven for 1 1/2 hours or until tender, basting every 15 minutes from 1/2 cup of the wine, using one of the huge-eye-dropper types of basters that is more efficient than a gingerly wielded spoon.

Finally, lying side by side on a hot platter, these still sputtering rabbits, garnished with watercress and shoestring potatoes, will draw your hunger around you like a cloak—especially when nearby a steaming gravy boat in which the remaining juices and 1/2 cup of boiling water, brought to a quick simmer in the roasting pan, promises added deliciousness.

COLD RABBIT LOAF

Here's a hot-weather luncheon or supper dish, as refreshing as an early morning in the spring. Start by bringing 4 pounds of rabbit and 1 1/2 quarts of cold water slowly to a bubble in your Dutch oven. Skim. Then add a diced onion, a diced carrot, a large sliced stalk of celery with the leaves, a sliced clove of garlic, 1 teaspoon salt, 1/8 teaspoon freshly ground black pepper, a bay leaf, and several sprigs of watercress. Cover and simmer 1 1/2 hours or until the meat is separating from the bones.

Remove the rabbit, and while it is cooling strain the stock. If there is more than a quart, boil it uncovered to that amount. Soften 2 tablespoons of gelatin in a little cold water and stir thoroughly into the seething stock.

Bone and dice the meat. Add to the stock and, tasting, correct the salt and pepper. Then pour into a casserole and allow to cool before setting in the refrigerator to chill and gel.

This is excellent with cold potato salad, begun by scrubbing and boiling 6 medium-size potatoes, removing them from the salted water while they are still hard, then peeling them as sparingly as possible to preserve the utmost flavor and nourishment. Hard-boil 6 eggs at the same time, then plunge them under cold water and peel them.

Slice some of the hot potato into an earthenware, glass, crockery, or stainless steel bowl. Slice some egg atop it. Now pour on a liberal amount of preferably olive oil or some good salad oil. Douse on about 1/4 as much vinegar. Salt

and pepper. Sprinkle on a very small amount of powdered garlic. Paprika and parsley flakes will add eye and taste appeal. Repeat, keeping on doing this until you've used all the potatoes and eggs. Cover so that the flavor will permeate everything.

Preparing this salad half a day or more ahead of time will give the best results. Take the lid off once or twice and carefully, so as not to break up the eggs and potatoes, spoon the mixture around a bit to redistribute the oil and vinegar.

RABBIT CASSEROLE

Slowly brown 3 pounds of rabbit, cut into serving pieces, with 1/2 stick of butter or margarine in a large frypan atop the stove. Then warm 1/4 cup applejack in a saucepan, set afire, and pour over the meat. Afterwards, fork out the rabbit and place to one side.

Add 1 1/2 cups diced onion, 1 cup diced carrot, and stir around over medium heat for half a dozen minutes. Now include 1/4 cup sliced mushrooms and cook another 3 minutes.

Remove from the stove long enough to stir in 1 1/2 teaspoons of tomato paste and 3 tablespoons of sifted flour that have already been blended into a smooth paste. Pour in a cup of hot water in which a chicken bouillon cube has been dissolved and 1/2 cup good dry sherry. Stir over low heat until everything comes to a bubble, season to taste with salt and freshly ground black pepper, and simmer for 3 minutes.

Transfer to a casserole, mix in the meat, sprinkle with grated Parmesan cheese and paprika, cover, and cook in a moderate 350° oven for 45 minutes or until the rabbit is tender. When you take the first enchanting taste, see if the earth doesn't rock a little under your feet.

ROAST RABBIT

For country-style roast rabbit to whet the taste buds you'll need about 3 pounds of the raw product. Wipe dry with several paper towels, then dust with 1 1/2 teaspoons seasoned salt, and 1/2 teaspoon apiece of poultry seasoning, fresh paprika, and parsley flakes.

Set, the back down, in a low, open roasting pan. Put a later discarded peeled onion, a celery stalk with the leaves, and a small clove of garlic in the cavity. Rub with 1/2 stick of half-melted butter or margarine. Roast in a moderate 325° oven for an hour or until tender.

To make the results really eloquent, and the smells soul-stirring, baste liberally every 10 minutes with a sauce made by simmering in a saucepan over low heat for 3 minutes a can of concentrated chicken broth, 1/4 cup good sherry, 1 teaspoon sugar, 1/2 teaspoon salt, 1/4 teaspoon dried rosemary, and 1/8 teaspoon freshly ground black pepper.

Bring to the table on a hot platter, surrounded by a dozen small new potatoes that have been scrubbed, cooked in boiling water for 1/2 hour or until tender, drenched with 1/2 stick of melted butter or margarine, and sprinkled with 1/4 teaspoon apiece of seasoned salt and dill seed. Even before you get to eating, drinking in the fragrance will be to your hunger like water to the thirsty.

CHARCOAL BROILED RABBIT

The first time we ever cooked this, on a California patio, I caught a glimpse of a bushy tail and a narrow mask in the cool black night shadows. Evidently the heady smell of his natural prey had brought the fox near the sputtering meat and the still, hushed circle of gleaming charcoal.

Marinade a brace of tender young 2-pound rabbits, cut and disjointed into serving pieces, all afternoon in the refrigerator in 1/2 cup olive oil, 1/4 cup of your favorite wine, 2 tablespoons choped parsley, a tablespoon finely chopped green onion, 1 teaspoon dried sage, 1/4 teaspoon freshly ground black pepper, 1/8 teaspoon apiece of tarragon and rosemary, and the juice of a crushed clove of garlic. Move the pieces several times, making sure that all parts of the meat come in contact with the mixture.

Over the glowing charcoal turn the pieces occasionally so that they cook evenly, at the same time brushing each anew with the marinade. About 45 minutes should find them juice-filled and tender, the crust crisp and the savor enchanting.

RABBIT CONTINENTAL

Place 3 to 4 pounds of rabbit or hare, enough to feed four, in a roasting pan with a cup of canned tomatoes, 1/2 cup of good dry sherry, a large diced onion, a sliced clove of garlic, a tablespoon of chicken fat or the equivalent of butter or margarine, a tablespoon of seasoned salt, and freshly ground black pepper and paprika to taste, all of which have been well mixed.

Roast 2 hours uncovered in a moderate 325° oven, spooning the sauce over the rabbit every 1/4 hour to keep the meat moist. This is good when the first blue shadows of evening lift across the dining room, keeping night at bay a little longer.

OLD WORLD RABBIT

As Brillat-Savarin remarked, the discovery of a new dish does more for the happiness of man than the finding of a star, and here perhaps is a way of preparing rabbit which you have not known before. Try it sometime with a 4 or 5-pound oldster that is too tough for ordinary treatment.

Set the granddaddy on a rack in a kettle. Pour in a quart of boiling water. Add 2 teaspoons seasoned salt. Bring to a bubble, lower the heat, and simmer until tender. Then cool in the broth.

While all this is going on, melt 2 tablespoons butter or margarine in a small heavy saucepan over low heat. Smoothly stir in 2 tablespoons flour, mixed to a thin paste with a little water. Once these are well blended, blend in slowly, bit by bit, a cup of whole milk. Continuing to stir, bring gradually to a bubble and simmer 2 minutes. Season to taste with salt and freshly ground black pepper, then with 1/4 teaspoon nutmeg. Combine this sauce with 1/2 cup whipped cream, 1/4 cup dry sherry, and 1 teaspoon Worcestershire. Place to one side.

Cook a large bunch of broccoli, drain, and arrange in a casserole. Dust with part of a cup of grated Parmesan cheese. The rabbit should now be cool enough to handle.

Bone it, spreading the pieces over the broccoli. Tilt and scrape the sauce over everything. Sprinkle on the rest of the cheese. Place 5 inches below the broiler and cook until bronzed and bubbly. The results will shine in your memory like a patch of old-world stained glass with the sun against it.

RABBIT SALAD

Here's a cold rabbit salad, perfect for a buffet meal, that'll make a day brighten up like cliff swallows swooping into the sunlight. While you're cutting 3 cups of cooked rabbit into small cubes, get enough water boiling in a saucepan to cover 4 eggs by an inch. Place the eggs in the pan with a spoon and let the temperature immediately drop to a simmer, keeping it that way for 8 to 10 minutes, making sure that the eggs remain covered with water all this time. Then remove from the heat and plunge into cold water. If the eggs are cracked slightly before they cool, peeling will be easier.

Chop the hard-boiled eggs into small bits. Then chop up 1 1/2 cups celery. Combine rabbit, eggs, and celery with 1/4 cup of the rabbit stock and 1 tablespoon cider vinegar, adding sufficient mayonnaise to hold the mixture together. Season to taste with salt and freshly ground black pepper. Decorate with paprika and have four chilled plates ready.

JACKRABBIT JAMBALAYA

The secret with these agile-legged bounders is to bone the meat before cooking it, thereby ridding it of a somewhat gamy taste that some find disagreeable. Then 2 cups of cooked, chopped jackrabbit will give you an enjoyable jambalaya.

Start by melting 2 tablespoons butter or margarine in a large, heavy frypan over low heat. Stir 2 tablespoons onion and 1 tablespoon apiece of parsley, celery, and green pepper, all finely chopped, in this until tender. Smoothly blend in 2 teaspoons of flour, first mixed into a thin paste with a little water, and cook until the flour is golden.

Add 2 cups of stewed tomatoes, a minced clove of garlic, 1/2 teaspoon salt, 1/4 teaspoon thyme, 1/8 teaspoon freshly ground black pepper, and only if you like what it can do for a dish either 1/4 or 1/8 teaspoon of chili powder, depending on your palate. Simmer until thick.

At the end stir in the jackrabbit and a cup of Minute Rice, smooth, cover, and continue to simmer very slowly, with only the occasional bubble plopping to the surface, for 5 minutes. You may be surprised to find this enchanting even the most delicate appetites.

RABBIT CACCIATORE

Dust 4 pounds of rabbit pieces with salt and freshly ground black pepper to taste, sprinkle with paprika, dredge in flour, shaking off any excess, and saute in 6 tablespoons of olive oil until golden. Then remove to a plate for the time being, keeping it warm.

Add 1/2 pound of mushrooms and a diced onion to the hot oil remaining in the frypan and saute until the mushrooms have shriveled and the onions are soft and tan. Then pour in a small can of tomatoes and 1/2 cup of good white wine. Bring to a simmer for 5 minutes, stirring occasionally, then return the rabbit and cook until it is warmed throughout.

Sprinkle in several sprigs of chopped parsley, a minced clove of garlic, and a tablespoon of brandy. Cover and cook over low heat until tender. Dot with 2 tablespoons of melted butter or margarine and serve with steaming white rice or spaghetti. It'll lift the heart.

SOUTHERN RABBIT

Here is a dish that will bring brightness to the table on a cool damp evening when, snow threatening, the moonlight is murky and indistinct under velvet clouds. Start it by frying 2 slices of bacon until crisp, starting with a cold frypan and then crumbling the pieces. Add 1/2 cup apiece of diced green pepper and diced onion, plus a finely sliced clove of garlic, and saute slowly over low heat, stirring and turning frequently so that the onions do not burn.

Then stir in 3/4 cup apiece of diced cooked rabbit and diced cooked ham with the fat removed. Saute a dozen minutes more.

Put in a cup of canned or freshly cooked tomato, 1 1/4 cups of chicken bouillon, 1/2 cup of washed raw rice, 1/2 teaspoon seasoned salt, 1/4 teaspoon thyme, 1/8 teaspoon cayenne pepper, and a bay leaf. Stir and cook a minute. Correct the salt and pepper if necessary.

Then spoon and pour into a large casserole, well greased with butter or margarine. Bake in a preheated moderate 350° oven an hour or until the rice is fluffy and most of the liquid is absorbed. Serve with hot, buttered sourdough toast.

HASENPFEFFER

Varying hare are so thick in the Peace River country of Northern British Columbia, where we have a log cabin, that on one occasion they dropped a tent in which I was sleeping by gnawing at the guy lines and on another freed a tethered saddle mare during the night by eating through her salt-encrusted picket rope in three places. This is the place where we have tried at least a dozen different recipes for hasenpfeffer. The following one has become my favorite.

You'll need about 4 pounds of rabbit, separated into serving pieces. Marinate these for 2 days refrigerated in a glass or earthenware or stainless steel container, first covering them with equal parts of red wine and mild vinegar, 2 cups sliced onion, 6 whole cloves, 4 bay leaves, 2 teaspoons salt, and a teaspoon apiece of thyme, dry mustard, tarragon, and freshly ground black pepper. Turn the meat when you get up in the morning and again before retiring.

Then wipe the rabbit dry, sprinkle with a little flour, and saute in a heavy saucepan or Dutch oven with a stick of butter or margarine until well tanned on all sides. Strain the marinade over the meat. Cover and let bubble over low heat for some 40 minutes or until the mildly flavored portions are tender. Correct the seasoning with more pepper and salt if this should prove necessary.

Remove the meat to a hot platter. Add a tablespoon of sugar to the liquid. Thicken with a thin paste concocted by smoothly mixing 6 tablespoons of flour with 3/4 cup of cold water. Bring again to a bubble and simmer, stirring, for several minutes. Then mix in a cup of sour cream. Once the bubbles start lifting through the gravy again, pour it over the rabbit and serve with steaming buttered noodles. Everything will have a smooth, sensuous taste.

RABBIT WITH CASHEWS

Cashews are sold in quantity in the open markets of Mocambique, and it was during a recent visit to Lourenco Marques that we obtained such a quantity of the freshly salted variety that since they have played a prominent part in our wild-game cookery. Their provocative flavor goes particularly well with the delicate woodland taste of young rabbit. You'll need about 3 pounds of these, separated into serving pieces.

Brown them in 2 tablespoons apiece of olive oil and butter or margarine. Then remove the meat and tilt the fat from your frypan. Then, scraping the pan to include the tasty browned bits, add 2 tablespoons of good brandy and stir around diligently. Add the contents of a can of condensed cream of chicken soup, 1/2 cup sour cream, a tablespoon chopped onion, 1/2 teaspoon monosodium glutamate, 1/4 teaspoon apiece of parsley flakes and paprika, and 1/8 teaspoon of freshly ground black pepper. Stirring, bring to a bubble.

Return the rabbit to the pan, cover, and simmer over low heat for 45 minutes or until nearly tender, stirring occasionally. Sprinkle in 1/2 cup of chopped cashews and keep bubbling 15 minutes more, uncovered so the sauce will thicken. Such a repast is as satisfying as a cascading run of Chopin.

AZTEC HASENPFEFFER

Here's a slightly different, somewhat Aztec, simplified, and delicious way to go about preparing a traditional dish that on this continent has been enhancing tables since they were hand hewn. Cut and disjoint a 3 to 5-pound rabbit or hare and let stand 2 hours before cooking in 2 cups of vinegar, moving it around every 1/2 hour.

When the meat is ready, dice a thick slice of salt pork and brown in a heavy frypan. Slice 2 large onions, dust with flour, and tan them with the salt pork. Put in the marinated meat and saute until lightly golden. Then add a cup of claret, 1/2 teaspoon salt, 1/8 teaspoon freshly ground black pepper, and a grated square of cooking chocolate. Cover and simmer 1 1/2 hours or until the meat is tender.

Now in a large saucepan, saute a dozen small white onions and 1/2 pound of mushrooms in 1/4 stick of butter or margarine until the onions are tender. Then fork the pieces of rabbit or hare in with them and strain the sauce from the skillet over everything. After simmering 5 minutes, this hasenpfeffer will be ready to serve with mashed potatoes, spaghetti, noodles, or whatever you favor with your cold beer.

ROSEMARY RABBIT

This dish has a uniqueness to it, like a full-rigged schooner in a glass bottle. Sprinkle some 3 pounds of tender young rabbit, disjointed and cut into serving pieces, with sifted flour seasoned with a teaspoon of salt, 1/8 teaspoon freshly ground black pepper, and a dusting of paprika. Brown evenly over low heat in a frypan with 1/4 cup of mixed olive oil and melted butter or margarine.

Then add 1/2 cup of your best white wine and a tablespoon of preferably fresh rosemary from your herb garden, finely chopped. If you have only dried rosemary, soak half that amount in the wine and substitute that. Cover and simmer for 1/2 hour or until just tender. Serve the meat on a hot platter with the sauce strained over it. A few sprigs of the fresh rosemary, if you have it, will make the little feet of the fragrance go one, two, three, skip.

RABBIT GUMBO

For a gumbo for the gods, add a medium-size carrot, a medium-size onion, and a small turnip, all sliced, to 6 cups of water in a large kettle and bring to a boil. Add 3 pounds of disjointed and cut-up rabbit. If necessary, pour in enough water to cover and continue to cook.

When the water is once more bubbling, stir in a teaspoon of salt, 1/2 teaspoon thyme, 1/4 teaspoon freshly ground black pepper, 4 sprigs of parsley, a bay leaf, and the freshly squeezed juice of 1/2 lemon. Reduce the heat until only the occasional bubble plops to the surface, cover, and cook 50 minutes.

Fork out the meat and put aside to cool. Drain the broth, discarding the solids. Boil the remaining liquid until it is reduced to 5 cups. As soon as you can handle it, bone the rabbit and dice the meat. You are now ready for the gumbo part of this table-gracing masterpiece.

Using your sharpest knife, cut a pound of ripe tomatoes and a medium-size onion into very thin slices. Then chop 3/4 pound of okra into 1/4-inch sections.

Melt 2 tablespoons of butter or margarine in your frypan. Smoothly blend in 3 tablespoons of sifted flour that have been mixed into a thin paste with a little water and, stirring, cook over low heat 3 minutes. Saute the sliced onion, stirring and turning, for 6 minutes or until the sputtering ceases. Then tilt in the tomato and okra and, stirring continually, saute for another half-dozen minutes or until the latter loses its stickiness. Continuing to wield your spatula, drop in a crushed clove of garlic and cook 2 more minutes.

Now turn the vegetables into at least a 3-quart saucepan, scraping the last vestiges of the flavor from the frypan with the help of a few splashes of the stock. Then pour in roughly 1/2 of the rabbit stock, add 2 teaspoons of salt, cover, and keep at a bubble for an hour, stirring occasionally.

The time has now arrived for the addition of the rabbit and the other 1/2 of the stock. Then put the lid back on and, stirring occasionally, simmer another 30 minutes.

Place 2 tablespoons of cooked white rice, colorfully dusted with paprika and parsley flakes, into each of a quartet of large heated soup plates. Portion the gumbo among the plates and start enjoying it immediately. The cooking of such a dish, besides bringing a flush to your cheeks, will put a sparkle in everyone's eyes, especially if there is also a crisply tossed green salad and the wine glasses are red with Burgundy.

SQUIRREL STROGANOFF

This one will have your guests lingering happily about the stove on which it is cooking and giving off good smells, and it is a tasty way to use the patriachs of the treetops. You'll need a pound of boned, ground meat.

Start by sauteing 1/4 cup of diced onion until tender only, not brown. Then stir in the meat, dust with 1/4 teaspoon of powdered garlic, and cook until lightly gold. At this time, lay 4 ounces of egg noodles over the squirrel and onions.

Mix a couple of 8-ounce cans of tomato sauce, a cup of water, 1/2 cup of dry red Burgundy, 1/4 cup sliced mushrooms, a tablespoon seasoned salt, and 2 teaspoons Worcestershire sauce. Pour over everything, bring to a bubble, cover, and simmer 1/2 hour or until the noodles, tested by biting, are just tender. Finally, stir in a cup of sour cream and bring back to a bubble for 3 minutes. By this time everyone's appetite will be as restless as the sea.

ISLAND FRIED SQUIRREL

This is by the way of being a meek dish, but satisfying. Marinate for 2 hours enough disjointed and cut-up young squirrels for four in a cup of soy sauce, a teaspoon powdered ginger, 1/2 teaspoon seasoned salt, 1/2 teaspoon garlic powder, and 1/4 teaspoon paprika.

Then drain the pieces thoroughly and roll them lightly in flour. Get 3 tablespoons apiece of shortening and butter or margarine very hot in a heavy, cast-iron skillet. Put in the pieces of squirrel, skin side down. Lower the heat immediately and fry, uncovered, until the meat is brown on one side. Turn the one and only time and brown the other side, the total operation taking some 35 to 40 minutes.

Remove the meat to absorbent paper to drain, keeping it in a warm place while you fry 8 slices of pineapple. The results will please the eye, gladden the palate, and edify the soul.

HASHED BROWN SQUIRREL

Here's something that'll keep your appetite as lively as a sandpiper skittering along the water's edge. Dice 1 1/2 cups of cooked squirrel. Put 1/4 stick of butter or margarine into a heavy frypan over low heat. While it is melting, mix the meat, 2 cups chopped boiled potatoes, 1/2 cup chicken bouillon, and 1 1/2 teaspoons minced onion. Season to taste with salt and freshly ground black pepper, then dust with enough paprika to give everything a rich appearance.

Using a spatula, spread this mixture evenly in the frypan and cook over very low heat for 1/2 hour or until golden on the bottom, stirring and lifting from the bottom occasionally to prevent sticking and to spread a crisp overtone throughout the hash. When brown underneath, slide out onto a hot platter. The smell of this cooking will make you as hungry as a gull.

SQUIRREL BROCHETTE

Once a major target of our buckskinned ancestors, the innumerable wild squirrel that now chatter their way through the trees of this continent still provide gourmet tidbits for hungry families, especially as like the rabbit they have little if any gaminess. The only difficulty is that there are those among us who maintain they've never tasted a tender squirrel, and it's certainly a fact the muscularity of the more mature members of these acrobatic troupes can be something to contend with. But even with the elders there is a delectable way around.

For the same quartet of diners for which all these recipes are designed, grind 2 pounds of lean, boned squirrel. Mix thoroughly with a cup of soft white bread crumbs, 3/4 cup chicken bouillon, 2 tablespoons finely chopped onion, 1 teaspoon salt, and 1/8 teaspoon paprika. Then mold into balls the size of small eggs.

Alternate on green-stick or metal skewers with quarters of unpeeled tomato, chunks of onion, and folded strips of bacon. Grill until golden. Who says that in North America, except maybe in Quebec, there are no real chefs except in the canneries?

ROAST SQUIRREL

Young squirrel, too many times overpowered by spices and sauces, have such a fragility of flavor that if you have a turning spit, you may choose to roast enough for four until just tender, adding nothing to their natural deliciousness except what may be imparted by basting them every dozen minutes with melted butter or margarine. The outcome is squirrel pristine and pure; uncorrupted, succulent, fresh, with a delicacy of treetop sweetness not otherwise to be won.

If there is no rotisserie where you are, roast the younglings in a low uncovered pan in a slow 325° oven, basting every 12 minutes with melted butter or margarine and the juices, until a sharp fork can be readily inserted in a thigh and as easily withdrawn.

SQUIRREL SUPREME

For a change of pace, bring to a simmer in a saucepan a cup of tomato catsup, 1/2 cup each of cider vinegar and currant jelly, and 1/2 teaspoon tarragon. Stir in 2 cups of chopped roast squirrel and keep bubbling 15 minutes. Season to taste with pepper and salt. Try this sometime with light, hot, flaky baking powder biscuits. It'll have a warm zestful charm which you're almost sure to find pleasing.

SQUIRREL RISOTTO

The sweet, velvety, short-fibered meat of the squirrel lends itself elegantly to this one-dish meal. Grind or chop up a cup of the meat and saute it in your frypan with a stick of butter or margarine until tender. Then remove the squirrel with a slotted spatula, large perforated spoon, or such and keep warm.

While this is going on, you'll have plenty of leisure in which to chop 1/2 cup each of onion and fresh mushrooms. Turn the onions into the grease first and stir until just tender. Then scatter in the mushrooms and saute 2 minutes more.

Tip in 2 1/2 cups of seething chicken bouillon unless you're blessed with the same volume of rabbit stock, thoroughly stir in a cup of Minute Rice, bring to a bubble, smooth, cover, and let stand over low heat for 5 minutes. Check for seasoning.

Then stir in the squirrel and 2 tablespoons of chopped watercress. Sprinkle with Parmesan cheese and serve immediately, although such a moment is so enjoyable that it's a shame to hurry it.

SQUIRREL AND RED WINE

While the grinder is still handy, put through it 1 1/2 pounds of lean, boned, older squirrel. Lightly mold into 4 thick patties. Marinate these all afternoon at room temperature in 3 cups of your best red wine and the juice of a crushed clove of garlic. Then drain and dry the cakes.

Melt 1/2 stick of butter or margarine in a heavy frypan over high heat, just short of burning, and quickly cook the burgers, preferably 2 minutes to a side although there will be those who prefer their meat less rare, and who is there to say that they are wrong. Smear lightly with prepared mustard, place on hot buttered toast, and keep warm.

Working rapidly, stir 1/4 cup of the marinade into the juices in the frypan, bring to a bubble, and pour over the hot squirrel patties. Devoured with the help of a knife and fork, they'll make the moment seem tall.

JULIENNE SQUIRREL SALAD

You'll need 3 cups of cold, boned, cooked squirrel, cut into long narrow strips. This meat will be moistest and most delicious if the squirrels have been consigned to a deep kettle, half-covered with salted bubbling water, then simmered with the lid on for 3 hours or until tender.

Blend 1/4 cup of mayonnaise with 2 tablespoons heavy cream, a tablespoon of freshly squeezed lemon juice, 1/4 teaspoon salt, and 1/8 teaspoon apiece of marjoram, parsley flakes, and newly ground black pepper. Mix thoroughly with the meat. Then arrange attractively on a cold platter with romaine lettuce that has been separated and washed leaf by leaf, radish slices, stuffed olives, and wedges of tomato. This is especially refreshing on a windless noon when the mists of autumn coil motionless in the hollows.

STUFFED WOODCHUCK SALAD

Woodchuck sharpshooting spells good eating as well as good sport, particularly if after skinning the trophies you carefully cut out the small, kernel-like glands from inside the forelegs. Young woodchuck are in the main tastiest roasted, and if there's some left over, here's a change of pace salad for a smoky afternoon.

Peel 4 firm, ripe tomatoes. Cut a thin slice from each top and spoon out the centers, saving the pulp but discarding as many seeds as possible. Dust the insides with salt, turn upside down on a plate, and place in the refrigerator for an hour.

While the tomatoes are thus chilling, cube 2 cupfuls of the cooked 'chuck. Sprinkle with the juice of 1/2 lemon, cover, and place in the refrigerator until the tomatoes are ready.

This will give you time to mix 2 tablespoons of sifted flour, 2 teaspoons sugar, a teaspoon dry mustard, 1/4 teaspoon parsley flakes, and 1/8 teaspoon cayenne in a heavy small saucepan. Stir smoothly and slowly into this 3/4 cup evaporated milk and 1/4 cup cider vinegar into which you've beaten an egg. Stir this constantly over low heat until everything has begun to thicken. Then mix thoroughly with the rest of the stuffing, along with 1/2 cup of the chopped tomato pulp.

Stuff the tomatoes and place each, on its separate plate, on a crisp bed of lettuce, surrounded with the equally apportioned remaining stuffing, all garnished with watercress. Eaten when the gentle afternoon sunshine in its pleasance also graces the table, this is unforgettable.

WOODCHUCK AND PASTA

A patriarch of the pastures will do admirably for this. Grind 1 1/2 pounds of lean meat. After you've wilted a large onion and a clove of garlic, both chopped, over low heat in your skillet with 2 tablespoons of olive oil, remove the vegetables and, stirring, separate and brown the meat. Then mix in the onion and garlic.

Cook 1/2 pound noodles until just tender, according to

the instructions on the packet, stir in both margarine or butter to taste, and in the same manner the usual salt and pepper. Grate a cup of Parmesan cheese.

Spread a layer of the noodles over the bottom of a greased casserole, then a layer of the meat and vegetables, and finally a layer of cheese dusted with oregano and paprika. Keep this up until everything is used.

Top with sauce made by emptying 2 small cans of tomato paste into a saucepan, stirring in 2 cups of simmering water, adding 1/4 teaspoon basil and 1/8 teaspoon apiece of sugar and garlic powder, and seasoning to taste with salt and freshly ground black pepper.

Served with crisp breadsticks and a fresh green salad whose olive oil and vinegar catches the candlelight, this will give dignity to the deep electric blue of the night, almost as if you were on a terrace in the Italian Alps where, above, a tiny puff clouds the rim of a jet-black buttress, giving life to the vision before the distant rumble of a snowslide confirms it.

BRAISED WOODCHUCK

The rabbit recipes in this book will, if tenderness is taken into account, do wonderful things for woodchucks, too. As for securing this worthy game, dependable sharpshooters can usually get permission to stalk a farmer's spread for the ravenous ground hog, especially as two pairs of these burrowers will happily digest a ton of alfalfa in a month. Clean and skin your booty as promptly as reasonable, removing the small, strong-tasting, kernel-like glands from inside the forelegs and along the backbone. Trim away any excess fat, especially in the very early autumn when the woodchuck are at their best.

If your 'chuck is too grizzled to roast in a low uncovered pan with salt, pepper, and butter or margarine in a moderate 325° oven for 1 1/2 hours or until tender, cut and disjoint 2 pounds.

Fry 4 slices of chopped bacon until crisp, then remove from the pan for the time being. Saute a large diced onion in the remaining grease until the bits are golden. Then set in the pieces of meat and, turning frequently, tan them lightly.

Now add a large minced onion, a small chopped sweet pickle, 1/2 cup of hot water in which a chicken bouillon cube has been disolved, a teaspoon each of salt and paprika, a crushed clove of garlic, 1/2 teaspoon parsley flakes, and the reserved cooked bacon. Bring to a very slow bubble, put on the lid, and cook over low heat for 2 hours or until the woodchuck is tender. Check the salt. Then stir in 1/2 cup of sour cream, heat just short of a simmer, and serve with the gravy and hot baking powder biscuits. This is almost as complicated as a bouillabaisse but equally worth your efforts.

WOODCHUCK SOUP

Sometimes woodchuck are particularly plentiful, and then, freezer full and friends sated, soup may be your last delectable resource. Relegate the bones and odds and ends of meat to a large kettle, cover with 1 1/2 quarts of cold water, add salt to taste, and let bubble for 2 1/2 hours or until the meat is free of the bones. Strain the stock, cool, and spoon off the fat. Rescue as much of the meat as you can. You'll need a pound of it for this soup; 5 cups of stock.

Return these amounts of stock and woodchuck to the kettle, adjust the salt, add 1/4 teaspoon freshly ground black pepper, stir in a cup of dried lentils, and simmer 15 minutes.

Dice 2 medium-size onions, brown in your frypan with 1 1/2 tablespoons butter, and then scrape the entire contents of the pan into the kettle. Bring to a boil, mix in a cup of long-grained raw rice, cover and, giving the thickening contents the occasional stir, simmer 20 minutes or until the rice is tender. Ladled out with either chopped watercress or parsley, this has a wonderous savor.

With a repast so rich, the accompaniment should be simple, perhaps crisp unsalted crackers with some cheese that has been taken out of the refrigerator in time to return to room temperature; robust Port Salut from France possibly, or mellow Edam from the Netherlands, or assertive chedder from our own continent.

WOODCHUCK SHASLIK

The sizzling results of this recipe are so delicious that, once you've relished plump young woodchuck as prepared, you may choose to try the same formula with other small game. Marinate in a covered bowl or crock all afternoon in the refrigerator 2 pounds of cubed meat, 1/2 pound sliced Canada bacon, 4 firm tomatoes cut into wedges, 2 large sliced onions, and a dozen mushroom caps.

For the marinade blend 1/2 cup olive oil, a freshly squeezed large lemon, 2 mashed cloves of garlic, 1 teaspoon onion salt, and 1/4 teaspoon apiece of freshly ground black pepper and basil. Uncover about every hour, long enough to mix and toss everything thoroughly.

Then alternate the little squares of woodchuck, the folded bacon, and the vegetables on smoothly trimmed green wands or metal skewers. Turning these so that all parts will brown evenly, broil until a slid-off cube of 'chuck proves tender to the teeth in all its sudden and unmatched delectability. Shaslik like this, especially in a patio or backyard where its fragrances lift to the soft lapis blue of the sky, is not so much cooked as orchestrated.

WOODCHUCK PATTIES

Grind, with 1/4 pound of salt pork, 1 1/2 pounds of cleaned and boned woodchuck from which all fat has been cut and discarded. Mix this with a cup of fine bread crumbs, a slightly beaten egg, 1/2 cup chopped parsley, 1/4 cup of finely chopped green onions, 1/4 cup chopped green pepper, a crushed clove of garlic, 2 teaspoons dried basil, 1 1/2 teaspoons seasoned salt, and 1/4 teaspoon freshly ground black pepper.

Shape lightly, so that the ingredients will not be too tightly packed, into 4 patties. Dip into a beaten egg, then brown on both sides in the frypan with 2 tablespoons of butter or margarine. At the same time preheat your oven to a moderate 350°.

Top each patty with a slice of bacon and bake 1 1/2 hours. Serve on a hot platter, covered with a can of concentrated cream of mushroom sauce diluted with 1/4 cup of dry sherry. The light fragrance of it all will rise above the polite chatter of the dining room and hang there appetizingly.

ROAST BEAVER

Moist dark roast beaver is reminiscent of Thanksgiving, both in taste and smell, especially if you've come by a youngster. With blanket beaver, so called because in pioneer times four of its round pelts could be traded for a large Four Point Hudson's Bay Company blanket, the meat if cooked this way should first be treated with a tenderizer or it will become tougher and stringier the longer you try to tame it with heat.

Your beaver is apt to be plump, particularly if it has come from an amply poplar-rimmed pond, but it's an easy matter to trim off all but enough fat to cut down on the chore of basting. If you like the zest of garlic, cut tiny slits in the meat and insert slivers of this herb. Rub with a little chopped chives, dried thyme, salt, and freshly ground black pepper.

Roast at an even, moderate temperature of 350° for 20 minutes a pound, or until a leg moves readily up and down, on a rack in a shallow pan, covered at first with aluminum foil. About an hour before the beaver is scheduled to be done, take away the foil, pour a cup of your best port into the pan, and baste the roast every 15 minutes with it and the juices.

Let the roast beaver stand on a hot platter, in the open-doored oven with the heat off, for 10 or 15 minutes before carving. This will give you time to concoct the gravy which you can readily do by pouring and scraping the juices into a saucepan, smoothly stirring in 3 tablespoons of flour first blended into a thin paste with a little water, adding 2 cups of hot water, correcting the seasoning, and finally stirring over low heat until everything comes to a bubble. Served in a gravy boat from which it can be tipped over the steaming slices, this will add magnificence to even the first full shimmer of moonlight.

BEAVER HASH

When you have about 1 1/2 pounds of roast beaver left over and would like a simple, substantial meal, grind or cube the meat. You'll also need to chop up 2 medium-size onions and 2 stalks of celery. Saute these vegetables in a tablespoon of vegetable oil in your frypan until they are soft. Then add the meat and stir until everything is well browned.

Mix in a cup of canned tomatoes and a cup of Minute Rice. Stirring occasionally, simmer over low heat 5 minutes. Season to taste with a few drops of Worcestershire sauce, and sound the gong. Such hash is as exciting as waking up in a strange city.

BEAVER TAIL PEA SOUP

The flat black tail of the beaver, with which it smacks the water to warn its companions of danger, is one of the unlikeliest of the world's gourmet delights. Subjecting this to dry heat, as in a moderately warm oven, will cause the rough skin to puff and peel, exposing a white, gelatinous meat. Although this will enhance a pot of homebaked beans, the way we have come to prefer it is in a pea soup.

Start by boiling the skinned tail in 3 pints of water until the meat falls away from the bone, then discarding the latter and cutting the meat into cubes. Save the stock for the soup.

The instructions on your packet of dried split peas will indicate how much, if any, presoaking is required. A cup of the brand we buy has first to be immersed in 1 1/2 quarts of the stock left over from boning the tail, for half a day in the kettle we are going to use. Then stir, bring to a boil, stir again while you are reducing the heat, cover, and keep bubbling 2 hours.

Thinly slice 1/2 pound of peeled potatoes. Chop a small stalk of celery, leaves and all. Peel and chop a medium-size onion. Stir all this with the cubed meat into the peas at the end of the initial 2 hours, along with 1/4 cup dry sherry, 1 teaspoon salt, 1/4 teaspoon freshly ground black pepper, and 1/8 teaspoon thyme.

Stirring now and then, simmer another 3 hours, and don't be perturbed if you've made what seems to be too much, as it is better when it has stood a day in a cold place and then been rewarmed. But even right away it is as promising as a mountain lake that stretches to the horizon, green as the forest near its rim and darker out from shore where it is misting in the sun.

BEAVERBURGERS

For a hearty meal, cut up 2 pounds of fat raw beaver and 3 scrubbed but unpeeled medium-size potatoes, mix, and run through the food grinder. Chop a medium-size onion and 1/4 cup parsley and blend these in. Using a light hand, shape into 4 patties the area of the buns you are going to use.

Broil on one side 2 inches from the heat for 4 minutes, at the same time toasting 4 split buns. Set, cooked-side down, on each of the buns, lay a thin slice of cheese atop each, dust with paprika, and return beneath the broiler until the cheese melts and spreads. These will make your appetite throb.

PORCUPINE STEW

"Many campers would pass up a porcupine, on which there is even a bounty in some places, and yet he is the purest of all vegetarians," the dean of the outdoor writers, Colonel Townsend Whelen, told me when we were writing our woodcraft book, *On Your Own In The Wilderness*. "My memory goes back to when Bones Andrews, one of the last of the old mountain men of the breed of Jim Bridger, and I were compelled to spend several weeks in a British Columbia region where there was no game. At the end of that time we had about the worst case of meat fever you can imagine. So we saddled up our little pack train and made tracks for higher altitudes and game country. On the way up I shot a porcupine. I skinned it, starting at the smooth underneath, and tied it to the back of my saddle.

"That night we made it into a stew. First, we cut it into pieces and boiled these an hour. Then we added a handful of rice, some salt, a dozen small dumplings of biscuit dough, and covered all that to boil 20 minutes longer. This was tall country. With air pressures lessening with the altitude, the higher you climb, the longer you have to boil. We finally finished by adding a little flour to thicken the gravy and by stirring in a teaspoon of curry powder.

"Then the two of us sat down and finished the whole pot at one sitting. That pot held 9 quarts and was full."

PORCUPINE MULLIGAN

In your own kitchen where more ingredients are handy, you can make more of a production of the quill pig. A tender young porky weighing 5 or 6 pounds is tastiest in this mulligan, although an oldster can be used, too. Trim off any excess fat, rendering it for future use as it makes an excellent shortening. Disjoint and cut enough pieces to feed four. Brown, depending on the plumpness, with as much butter or margarine as may be necessary, preferably in a heavy, cast-iron Dutch oven.

Add 2 cups water, 1 cup Burgundy, the juices of a lemon, a diced clove of garlic, 2 bay leaves, 2 teaspoons salt, 1/4 teaspoon freshly ground black pepper, and 1/8 teaspoon apiece of powdered cloves, ground nutmeg, allspice, and paprika. Clang on the lid and keep at a bubble for 1 1/2 hours or until the meat is nearly tender. Then adjust the salt if necessary and fish out the bay leaves.

You'll have had plenty of time to have a quartet apiece of potatoes, onion, and celery stalks, all medium-size, sliced and ready. Stir these in, return the cover, and continue to simmer another 20 minutes or until the potatoes are tender, all of which will add to a growing feeling of contentment and good will.

PORCUPINE PATE

A principal cause why the waddling pincushions, like the equally unlovely ling which swim below our Peace River log cabin and which some scientists have told me are living fossils, are sought by the more catholic gourmets lies in their surprisingly big livers. For a particularly unusual and provocative pate, good for an entree along with mashed potatoes and a zesty green salad, cut about 1/2 pound of either liver into thin slices.

Chop 3 pieces of not-too-salty bacon and saute over medium heat with 1/2 stick of butter or margarine in a heavy frypan. As soon as you have enough grease to work with, add and tan a large diced onion. Then put in the liver for 12 minutes or until it is cooked throughout.

Run the solid ingredients through your grinder. Pour in the drippings from the frypan. Stir in 1/2 teaspoon monosodium glutamate, 1/8 teaspoon apiece of freshly ground black pepper and paprika. Continuing to sample carefully as you proceed, add salt to taste; 1/2 teaspoon or more depending on the bacon.

Now either put what you have through a blender or rub through a sieve, scrape and press firmly into a dish with the help of a rubber spatula, seal in the flavor with a fine topping of melted butter or margarine, and refrigerate until the next day. Dusted with parsley flakes, the end result will guarantee you a meal as luxurious as cut-glass wine goblets and sterling silver candlesticks.

ROAST RACCOON

If after skinning your raccoon you take care to cut out the exceedingly bitter, bean-shaped, kernel-like scent glands from the muscles under the front legs and each thigh, and if you'll substitute strips of salt pork for the sometimes strongly tasting natural fat, you'll end up with a savory feast reminiscent both in flavor and texture of the moist dark portions of chicken.

Roast coon, which requires about 3 hours in a slow 300° oven, is famous, particularly when the drippings of the liberally barded little trophy are run over it every 1/2 hour with the help of a bulb-type baster.

Then remove the roast, place on a hot platter in the oven with the heat shut off, and prepare a simple but sumptuous gravy by stirring a cup of simmering chicken bouillon into the drippings in the pan, adding enough flour first mixed to a thin paste with a little water to thicken everything to your liking, and seasoning to taste. Serve with baked sweet potatoes, boiled broccoli and butter, and crisp green salad dressed with vinegar and olive oil, while in the small yellow glow from the freshly lit fireplace the azure shadows flee from the dining room and amass themselves outside.

RACOON SHISH KEBAB

For shish kebab with a difference, cut 1 1/2 pounds of fat-trimmed coon into walnut-size cubes. Spread with 3 finely minced medium-size onions, 1 teaspoon paprika, 1/4 teaspoon thyme, and salt and freshly ground black pepper to taste. Keep covered in the refrigerator all afternoon.

When the day has finally faded, leaving a sky pinpricked with light against which the silhouettes of surrounding patios and homes make detailed outlines as sharp as if they had been scissored out of Victorian black velvet, skewer the meat and broil it evenly over hot coals.

Have 2 cans of concentrated beef broth and 2 cups of water simmering in a saucepan. Once the meat is tender unskewer it into the broth, bring to a bubble over moderate heat, and cook 12 minutes. The results will bring to some minds what Shakespeare said of Cleopatra, "She makes hungry where she most satisfies."

MUSKRAT CHILI

Here's a glorification of the lowly bean by a blend of musquash, like a strain from the G minor Bruch. Grind a pound of lean muskrat, press lightly into balls no bigger than marbles and, rolling them about, bronze with a teaspoon of cooking oil and another of butter or margarine in your largest skillet. Then, not disturbing the hot grease and juices, remove the meatballs for the time being.

Chop 3 medium-size onions, a large pepper, and 4 cloves of garlic. Stir the pleasantly odiferous trio around in the hot grease and muskrat oozings until the vegetables are soft but not browned.

Then add 3 sliced medium-size tomatoes, 1 tablespoon chili powder, 1/2 teaspoon cumin seed, and 1/2 teaspoon paprika. Return the meatballs. Mix thoroughly and then put in salt and freshly ground black pepper to taste. Keep at a bubble over low heat for about an hour or until thick.

At this point stir in a 1 pound can of chili beans, take off the heat, cover, and when cool stow in the refrigerator for 1 or 2 days. When you reheat it to serve, along with crisp crackers, you'll find the miraculously improved flavor will be a trumpet call to the appetite.

MUSQUACH MOUSSE

Soften 1 1/2 tablespoons of plain unflavored gelatin — probably from a tightly covered 1-pound box as this will be cheaper and more convenient than buying 1-tablespoon envelopes — in 3 tablespoons of cold water for 5 minutes.

While you're waiting, beat 2 egg yolks lightly and briefly and stir with 1/2 teaspoon apiece of salt and dry mustard, and 1/8 teaspoon each of paprika and cayenne, in the top of a double boiler whose lower half, sufficiently filled with water, you are bringing to a bubble.

Add to the egg and seasoning a cup apiece of beef bouillon and whole milk. Dust a few gratings of nutmeg over the top. Stirring continually, cook over the hot water until thickened.

Stir the results into the gelatin, continuing to mix until the latter is all dissolved. Then add 2 cups of chopped cooked muskrat, 1 tablespoon chopped parsley, 1 teaspoon cider vinegar, and the juice of a crushed clove of garlic. Cover and transfer to the refrigerator.

When it has started to thicken, fold in 1/2 cup of heavy cream that you've whipped to a light and frothy state. Spoon into 4 individual molds and chill till firm.

Unmold on 4 cold plates after letting the containers stand 1/2 minute in warm water nearly deep enough to cover them, then starting the severance by loosening the edges with a sharp, slender knife. Garnish with tender young watercress that has been washed in ice water. The results will be as grand as the sky, now clear, now piling up into vast monoliths of Pacific cloud.

SPIRITED LYNX

For an adventure in eating, enjoy lynx which, except for a stringiness in older animals, has the appearance and delicate savor of white chicken meat. Brown 2 pounds of cubed lynx with a stick of butter or margarine in a heavy frypan over low heat, tossing and turning the pieces until they are pale gold. Then lower the heat even more, salt and pepper moderately, and cook about 1/2 hour or until tender.

Blend 2 tablespoons each of dry sherry, Metaxa brandy, Kirsch, Madeira, port, and Canadian Club. Drench the meat with this and bring to a bubble for 3 minutes. Then, using a slotted spatula or perforated spoon, move the lynx to an already hot casserole, set on the lid, and place in a preheated moderate 325° oven until you can prepare the sauce.

For this, pour 1/4 cup of heavy cream into the spirits and juices remaining in the hot frypan. Stir thoroughly, just short of a bubble, for 2 or 3 minutes before straining into a saucepan over very low heat. Beat 2 egg yolks with 1/2 cup of heavy cream, add to the saucepan, and stir continuously, still keeping below a simmer, until thick.

Pour over the lynx, sprinkle with a tablespoon of chopped watercress and 1/2 teaspoon paprika, and serve with whipped potatoes, steaming baking powder biscuits, yellowly buttered noodles, or hot rice. This has a fragrant, frail elegance, far removed from what anyone would expect of wild game.

HOT LYNX SALAD

The lily-white, entirely non-gamy, delicately delicious cooked meat of the lynx lends itself admirably to this conversation-piece salad, hearty enough for a substantial luncheon. You'll need 2 cups of diced meat. Warm it and a cup of diced, then well-drained, pineapple 1/2 hour in the covered top of a double boiler.

Remove the lid long enough to stir in a cup of mayonnaise. Warm half a dozen minutes, using the hiatus to dice 1/2 cup celery, sliver or chop 1/2 cup of salted almonds, and dice 1/4 cup of green pepper. At the end of the 6 minutes, pick up your fork again and stir in the celery and 1/2 of the nuts.

Spoon the steaming salad in a mound on a hot platter. Sprinkle with the diced green pepper, the remainder of the almonds, and 1/4 teaspoon paprika. Garnish with watercress and quartered maraschino cherries. The result will cheer the room with its presence.

LYNX ASPIC

As with all the lynx recipes, this also makes a feast with cougar, and it has a sumptuous simplicity that'll titillate even those who've savored most of the familiar pleasures of the world. Pour into a small saucepan 1/2 cup of cold water and 1/4 cup of freshly squeezed lemon juice. Sprinkle on the tablespoon of gelatin contained in 1 envelope and stir over low heat until it dissolves.

Stir in 1/4 cup of stiffly whipped heavy cream, cover so that none of it will pick up any off flavors, and place in the

refrigerator. Once the mixture starts to thicken, add a cup
of the cooked white meat that has been cut into cubes and 2
tablespoons of chopped parsley. Salt to taste and include
1/2 teaspoon of paprika for added color, flavor, and
vitamins. Mold and chill, perhaps in 4 separate already cold
molds, and serve on crisp lettuce.

LYNX AND CHEESE

Cut eight 1/4-pound slabs from your preferably young
lynx, rub with 1 teaspoon seasoned salt and 1/8 teaspoon
freshly ground black pepper, dip each piece in a bowl of
beaten egg, roll in a cup of seasoned bread crumbs, and refrigerate for at least 1/2 hour.

When you're ready to go, bring 1/4 cup of cooking oil and
a stick of butter or margarine to a sizzle in your heavy
frypan. Then sear the lynx, lower the heat, and saute until
golden.

Add a cup of boiling water to a large casserole, assemble
the meat in one layer, season with 2 teaspoons oregano and
1 teaspoon apiece of garlic salt, basil, and paprika. Roof all
this with slices of Port Salut cheese, each topped with a
tablespoon of tomato sauce. Scatter 1/4 cup of grated
Parmesan cheese over the lot, slide the casserole uncovered
into a moderate 350° oven, and bake 50 minutes.

Garnish with watercress and set on a mat in the center of
the table, accompanied by a steaming bowl of brown and
wild rice, while beyond the terrace hungry rooks are
perhaps lifting their rusty voices.

LYNX AND DUMPLINGS

For lynx, cougar, or rabbit as delicate as a figurine, cut 2
pounds of the boned, white-cooking meat into pieces and
cover with boiling water. Add a teaspoon salt, 1/2 teaspoon
paprika, and 2 halved stalks of celery, leaves and all. Keep

at a bubble 2 hours or until pleasantly tender. Then take out all the celery.

Only then pour 3/4 cup of milk into a previously mixed 2 cups of flour, 1 tablespoon double-action baking powder, and 1 teaspoon salt into which a tablespoon of butter or margarine has been worked. Mix everything together very lightly and swiftly, using a folding motion.

Immediately place a single layer of rounded tablespoons of the batter in the broth bubbling atop the meat. Cover at once and allow the dumplings to steam for 15 to 20 minutes, whereupon they should be light and feathery. To keep them this way, serve them on a separate hot plate. Such a meal in the olden days would have filled you with the same sort of verve that in the Middle Ages started more than one Crusader toward the Holy Lands.

COUGAR

Among some of the tribes of aboriginal Americans who depended on wild meat, cougar was relished more than any other game. Like lynx, it has no gamy flavor at all. If you ever have the opportunity to try some, a sound way to begin is by cutting 2 pounds of the meat into 1/2-inch cubes. Cover these with real churned buttermilk for 1 1/2 hours. Then pour off the buttermilk and scatter the bits on crumpled absorbent paper to drain for 5 minutes.

Sift 1/2 cup of white flour into a paper bag and mix with a teaspoon salt, 1/4 teaspoon apiece of parsley flakes and paprika, and 1/8 teaspoon freshly ground black pepper. Funnel in the cubes, which still should be slightly damp, and shake the bag until they are well coated.

Heat 3 tablespoons apiece of cooking oil and butter or margarine in your heavy frypan, stir the cougar around until the bits are uniformly golden, cover, and allow to bubble for 1/2 hour or until tender. Then set the lid aside and cook another 7 minutes to bewitch the tidbits with compliments of flavorful crispness.

chapter four

OTHER NATURAL MEATS

THIS NEW WORLD grew up eating wild foods. Today, with trout and deer even thicker in many parts of the continent than during log-cabin days, one out of every five North Americans hunts, fishes, or does both.

Nearly everyone throws back to some degree to the characteristics of his caveman ancestors and, on occasion, finds satisfaction in living for a time as a primitive being. But hunting seasons are often short and the times between all too long. Then most of us must again depend on the butcher. But this is all the more reason to get the best, too, out of the meats he has to offer.

BEEF STEAK

Try to get a top grade, corn fed, fat marbled, light cherry red, boneless, 2-inch-thick, 2-pound sirloin steak that has been aged 4 or 5 weeks in the cooler. Whether the fat is yellow or white is unimportant, but the insides of the steer's bones should be red and porous, indicating that the animal was young.

Settle for wiping the steak with a clean damp cloth. Then rub the meat with your idea of enough salt and freshly ground black pepper. Using some of the discarded fat, rub your grill to avoid sticking. Preheat the broiler at a high temperature for 12 minutes.

Lay the steak 5 inches beneath the flame, searing each side rapidly to conserve as much as possible of the natural juices. For rare meat, most nutritious and therefore best if you like it, broil 10 minutes on each side. Medium takes an additional 5 minutes a side and well-done another 5 minutes on each side. Do not knife on your slab of butter or margarine until the cooking is finished. Serve the slices on hot plates while the meat is still sputtering.

BRAISED BEEF

Marinate a 4-pound top round of beef for 1 1/2 days in the refrigerator, lifting the cover and forking it over several times, in 1/2 cup olive oil, 1/2 cup dry sherry, 1/4 cup tarragon vinegar, a minced medium-size onion, a thinly sliced carrot, a finely chopped stalk of celery with the leaves, 2 dozen crushed peppercorns, a diced clove of garlic, 6 sprigs parsley, a bay leaf, a teaspoon paprika, and 1/8 teaspoon each thyme and rosemary. Finally, take out the beef and wipe it dry. Strain and keep the marinade.

Lard the meat with a 1/2 pound of fat and cold salt pork that you have sliced into long thin strips. Your butcher may be obliging enough to do this for you, or you can use a big larding needle to thread the slim lengths of fat through the lean beef at right angles to its grain, later cutting off any parts that protrude beyond the surface.

Brown the meat all over in 1 1/2 tablespoons butter or margarine in the bottom of a Dutch oven. Then warm 1/4 cup Metaxa brandy, set it afire, and tilt it over the beef. When the short-lived flames have abated, fork out the beef for the time being.

Now smoothly blend 3 tablespoons of flour with a teaspoon of tomato paste and add this to another melted 1 1/2 tablespoons of butter or margarine in the preferably heavy, cast-iron receptacle. Stir in the strained marinade, 1/2 can of concentrated beef broth, and any necessary salt and freshly ground black pepper. Bring to a rolling bubble, cover, and keep simmering 2 hours or until fork tender.

Set the fragrant chunk of meat on a hot platter, garnished with mushrooms and parsley, and cut about 1/2 of it into thin slices, drenching these with a generous amount of the strained gravy and serving what's left of the pleasantly odiferous liquid in a gravy boat.

BAKED LAMB CHOPS

This way of baking thick, prime, loin lamb chops will add deliciousness to even these widely desirable tidbits. Arrange 4 such carefully chosen chops in a low open pan along with a large, firmly ripe tomato cut into 8 wedges and a large sliced brown onion.

Blend 1 1/2 teaspoons salt, 1/2 teaspoon oregano, 1/4 teaspoon paprika, 1/4 teaspoon freshly ground black pepper, and 1/8 teaspoon parsley flakes and sprinkle over the meat. Then barely cover with water and slide into a moderate 375° oven for 45 minutes. afterwards, turn the meat and bake 1/2 hour more. Serve the then delectable liquid as the gravy.

BRAISED LEG OF LAMB

Cut away all excess fat and strip as much as possible of the parchmentlike membrane from a small 4 or 5-pound leg of lamb. Insert a clove of garlic in the meat at the shank. Then brown with a melted stick of butter or margarine, in a Dutch oven, turning the lamb to reach all sides.

Dust lightly all over with garlic salt, freshly ground black pepper, and paprika. Sprinkle with 1/4 cup chopped parsley and add 2 later-removed bay leaves. Then pour on

1/2 can concentrated beef broth into which you've stirred a teaspoon thyme. Cover snugly and simmer slowly, still atop the stove, for 3 hours.

Then interrupt the braising only long enough to pour most of the liquid into a small saucepan where you can thicken it by simmering it uncovered. Spoon off as much of the fat as possible.

Meanwhile, add 2 cups of halved and pitted green olives and 3 tablespoons butter or margarine to the bubbling contents of the Dutch oven, stirring the olives well in the juices.

Serve the lamb sliced on a hot platter, garnished with the olives and fresh sprigs of parsley and drenched with the saucepan of steaming, reduced deliciousness.

BROILED PORK TENDERLOIN

Cut a pork tenderloin, perhaps the choicest portion of the pig, crossways into inch-thick slices, rub lightly with a little freshly ground black pepper, and pan broil slowly over a low heat for about 1/2 hour or until very tender, turning it at short intervals so that it will brown evenly. Garnish it with melting butter or margarine, chopped parsley, and a bright dusting of paprika.

Timing it so that they'll be done at the same time, peel 4 bananas, scatter 1/2 teaspoon brown sugar and a bit of grated lemon peel atop each, set in a low well-greased pan, and bake in a moderate 350° oven 15 or 20 minutes or until the fruit begins to puff and blister on top. It'll really set off the savor of the sputtering pork.

ROAST PORK LOIN

Get a 4-pound center cut of loin, preferably with firm, fine-grained, whitish meat and firm white fat, planning to roast it the day it is brought home from the butcher's shop. First, though, have that worthy saw through the bone so that the cooked chunk can be carved more easily.

Rub salt and freshly ground black pepper generously into the roast before setting it, fat side up so that it will be self-basting, in a roasting pan. Lay thinly sliced onion over the top. Roast in a moderate 350° oven for 3 hours. For added delectability, serve hot applesauce.

STUFFED CHICKEN BREASTS

These were first served to us by Canadian artist and world-traveler Michael John Richmond in, of all places, his neighboring Hudson Hope log cabin. Mike's recipe is for eight diners, but that's all right as the stuffed chicken breasts, of which you'll need 1/2 breast per serving, are equally good cold. Leave the skin on the breasts. You'll also need 8 slices of thinly cut cooked ham.

Bone the chicken breasts or have your butcher do it. If the breasts are whole, cut them in half. Smash each halved breast with the side of a cleaver until quite flat.

Blend 1/2 cup butter, 1/2 cup chopped fresh mushrooms, 1/4 cup chopped fresh parsley, 1/4 cup chopped green onions, 1 teaspoon salt, another of freshly ground black pepper, and 1/8 teaspoon powdered garlic. Shape the resulting mixture into 8 little butter balls. Freeze these.

Lay a strip of ham over the filleted breast, enclose a frozen butter ball, roll the meat tightly around it, and secure shut with toothpicks. Place the stuffed breasts snugly together in a chilled dish in the refrigerator or ice box until ready to use.

Then dip the cold stuffed breast into flour, beaten egg, and finally fine bread crumbs in that order. Drop into hot fat and deep fry for 8 to 10 minutes, until well browned. Serve the first round at once. See if they aren't as wonderful as a first kiss.

CHICKEN A LA KING

Melt 1 1/2 sticks of butter or margarine, or preferably, 3/4 cup of chicken fat, in your heavy, cast-iron frypan.

Saute for 5 minutes 1 cup diced mushrooms and 1/4 cup diced pimento. Pour in a cup of heavy cream and another of whole milk and heat, stirring, short of a bubble.

Smoothly blend 1/2 cup of sifted flour into a thin paste with a little water and slowly add this to the contents of the frypan, all the time stirring. Season with 2 tablespoons salt and 1/8 teaspoon white pepper. Cook over low heat, always short of a simmer, until the sauce thickens. Then stir in 2 1/2 cups of diced cooked chicken and heat for serving, garnished with parsley and egg slices. If you find yourself preparing this often, the addition of 3 tablespoons of your best sherry just before it goes on the table will on occasion provocatively touch up the flavor.

ARROZ CON POLLO

For chicken and rice with a difference, disjoint about a 3 1/2-pound chicken and saute the pieces slowly in a large frypan with 1/2 cup olive oil until golden brown. Warm 2 tablespoons of dry sherry in a small saucepan, touch a match to it, and drench the chicken with this. Then add 3 finely diced medium-size green peppers, a finely diced medium-size white onion, and a mashed clove of garlic. Simmer everything gently until the onions are brown. Stir in 2 peeled and diced medium-size fresh tomatoes and cook 3 more minutes.

Then move everything into a well-greased casserole or baking dish that can later be transferred to a pad in the center of the table. Add a quart of chicken broth, 2 cups of long grain rice, and the merest pinch of saffron. Salt to taste and include 1/8 teaspoon red pepper. Then stir carefully with a wooden spoon, working from the rim toward the center without removing the spoon until you're finished, this to avoid breaking up the rice. Bring to a boil atop the stove. Cover and set in a moderate 350° oven for an hour.

To decorate this truly memorable dish, at the end remove the cover and arrange attractively over the top of the steaming delectableness 6 tablespoons of freshly simmered green peas, a tablespoon of chopped parsley, and 8 slices of pimento.

TURKEY TETRAZZINI

Saute with a stick of butter or margarine in your frypan 1/2 cup of thinly sliced mushrooms until lightly browned. Add 2 cups cooked turkey strips, 2 tablespoons dry sherry, 1 cup turkey stock, 1 cup heavy cream, the merest pinch of grated nutmeg, and salt and freshly ground black pepper to taste. Stirring over low heat, bring to a point just short of a simmer.

Blend 2 tablespoons of flour and an equal amount of butter or margarine into a smooth paste. Stir this, bit by bit, into the steaming turkey mixture. Continuing to stir, cook 5 minutes with no more than the occasional bubble plopping to the surface.

You'll need to boil 1/2 pound of thin spaghetti in salted water until tender but still firm to the bite, according to the directions on the package, first bending it gradually into the pot of hot liquid so that it will remain long. Drain in a colander. Then coil in a buttered, shallow casserole or baking dish that can be taken to the table.

Add the turkey mixture. Sprinkle with 3/4 cup of freshly grated Parmesan cheese. Bake in a preheated moderate 375° oven for 1/2 hour or until temptingly golden.

TURKEY AND ALMONDS

Mix 3 tablespoons flour into a thin paste with a little cold water and, stirring, blend smoothly with 2 tablespoons of melted butter or margarine, 1/4 teaspoon salt, and 1/8 teaspoon of freshly ground black pepper. Pour in 1/2 cup turkey stock and bring to a simmer. Then remove from the heat and stir in 1/2 cup regular cream. Break up an egg with a fork and add that.

Mixing as you proceed, add in order 1 tablespoon diced onion, 1 tablespoon finely chopped parsley, 1/8 teaspoon celery salt, 1/8 teaspoon paprika, 1/2 cup soft white bread crumbs, 1/2 cup slivered almonds, 1/4 cup sauteed sliced mushrooms, and 2 cups finely chopped cooked turkey.

Once everything is thoroughly blended, put into 4 large, buttered custard cups or similar containers, set these in a low flat pan of hot water, and bake in a moderate 325° oven 1/2 hour.

ROAST GUINEA HEN

A 4-pound guinea hen, next door to game in flavor, can be exceedingly good when roasted if properly seasoned and larded. Your butcher, especially as in most markets such a bird is a special event, may help matters along for you by sticking little slivers of fat in the breast. Lacking this, at least shove a chuck of salt pork into the cavity after rubbing the bird well inside and out with salt and freshly ground black pepper, truss the legs close to the body, arrange on a rack in a roasting pan, and drape several strips of salt pork over the top.

Roast uncovered in a moderate 325° oven for an hour or until fork-tender. For that crowning fillip, when the guinea hen is established at the table on a hot platter on its bed of steaming wild rice and 1/2 cup pinons, warm 1/4 cup of brandy in a small saucepan, set afire, and pour over everything.

GUINEA HEN PARMESAN

This is for that special foursome, as the subtly gamy guinea hen is usually both rather expensive and difficult to find, often having to be especially ordered. You'll need the boned and skinned breasts of 4, browned on both sides with 1/2 stick of butter or margarine in an oven proof pan you can cover. Once the meat is bronzed, add 8 fresh sliced mushrooms, put on the lid, and slide into a preheated hot 400° oven for a dozen minutes.

Afterwards, pour over the cooked fowl a sauce you've made by stirring and heating a cup of heavy cream and a jigger of your best sherry in a saucepan for 3 minutes, then removing it from the stove and thickening it by beating in an egg yolk. Sprinkle the birds with 1/2 cup of freshly grated Parmesan cheese, dust liberally with parsley flakes and paprika, and brown under the broiler.

Have ready 4 slices of lightly browned, cooked, smoked ham and 4 large slices of sourdough bread, cut 1/2-inch thick and sauteed in 1/4 stick butter or margarine until golden on both sides. Arrange the sourdough slabs on a hot platter. Place a slice of ham atop each. Then spoon on each portion of the guinea hen, mushrooms, and sauce. Serve at once, while the bread is still crisp.

DOMESTIC DUCK A L'ORANGE

Domestic duck is a far different article from the whistle-winged wild bird you finally manage to bag from a blind, and when roasting one, for example, you'll want to prick the skin periodically with your fork to let the excess fat escape.

For a domestic duckling for this recipe, one weighing about 5 pounds, rub it well with freshly ground black pepper, paprika, and salt and place a segmented orange in the cavity before consigning it to a rack in your roasting pan and setting it, uncovered, in a moderate 325° oven. Roasting it some 20 minutes per pound will be right, at the end of which time the drumsticks should wiggle easily, and when you jab it with a fork, the emerging juice will not be pink. Meanwhile, be periodically removing the excess grease so that its level does not meet the meat.

When the fowl is almost done, pour off all that remains of the accumulated fat and daub the top of the bird with a mixed 1/4 cup apiece of maple syrup and frozen concentrated orange juice. Turn up the oven heat 50° and let the bird glaze in it for 20 minutes.

While the oven activities are going on, keep the neck and the sliced giblets with the exception of the liver, bubbling in salted water to cover. This will give you a savory broth by the time you are ready to concoct the sauce. Also, peel a ripe thin-skinned orange, cut the rind into slivers, boil these 12 minutes in enough water to cover, and then scatter them on absorbent paper to drain.

Prepare the sauce by bringing to a simmer what's left of the 12-ounce can of frozen orange juice concentrate, 1 cup of some tart jelly such as currant, and 1 cup of the strained giblet broth, stirring until everything is dissolved. Add a tablespoon of lemon juice, a teaspoon powdered ginger, and the slivered rind, and simmer 3 minutes more. Serve everything hot, the pieces and slices of delectably glazed duckling streaming with the sauce.

DOMESTIC DUCK CASSEROLE

Rub a duckling, weighing about 5 pounds, inside and out with freshly ground black pepper, seasoned salt, and paprika. Set on a rack in a roasting pan and relegate to a hot 425° oven until it bronzes, pricking it occasionally with a fork to let the melting fat escape, all the time watching the bird carefully to make sure it does not burn.

Then, pouring off and saving for other cooking needs the accumulated grease, add a medium-size minced onion, a medium-size chopped carrot, a thinly sliced stalk of celery, a crushed clove of garlic, a bay leaf, and 1/8 teaspoon thyme. Lower the heat to a moderate 325° and cook an hour. Then take out the duckling and allow it to cool enough so that you can quarter it. Put these quarters on a hot platter in the oven with the heat shut off.

In the meantime, simmer the giblets except for the liver (which you can enjoy as a separate reward, sauteed for a minute on each side in a tablespoon of butter or margarine) and the neck in enough lightly salted water to cover. Drain the results into another saucepan and boil down the liquid, if necessary, to 1 cup. Discard the neck, first removing what meat you can and chopping this and the giblets. Blend 2 tablespoons sifted flour smoothly with 2 tablespoons of the melted duck fat. Add the chopped giblets and the flour paste to the stock and simmer, stirring, until the resulting gravy thickens.

Brown 8 small white onions with 2 tablespoons of the reserved duck fat in the bottom of a casserole. Add a package of frozen green peas, a shredded half of a heart of crisp lettuce, 2 cups boiling water, a tablespoon of sugar, and 1/2 teaspoon seasoned salt. Bring to a bubble, cover, and cook 1/2 hour. Then take off the heat, dust with paprika, and fold in 1/2 stick of butter or margarine.

Bring the platter of hot roast duckling out of the oven. Surround it with the vegetables from the casserole, and pour the gravy over the bird. Serve with applesauce.

CRUNCHY, CRISPY CORNISH GAME HEN

Take 4 of the little game hens and lightly butter them. Then roll them in a mixture of prepared stuffing mix that has been mashed into crumbs with a rolling pin and reinforced with 5 tablespoons Parmesan cheese and 2 tablespoons parsley flakes. Slide into a preheated hot 400° oven and bake until brown and tender—some 45 to 50 minutes. The results will be delectably crisp and crunchy.

BETTY BROWN'S ROCK CORNISH GAME HEN

Here is a favorite of ours that our good friend Betty Brown serves at least once for her lieutenant colonel husband and us whenever we are visiting their home, Seawynd, on Puget Sound. Before placing the 4 tiny fowl in pans, Betty soaks them 1 1/2 hours in salted water.

Then she blends 1 1/2 sticks butter, 2 tablespoons seasoned salt, 1 tablespoon onion powder, 1 1/2 teaspoons basil, 1 1/2 teaspoons rosemary, 1 1/2 teaspoons paprika, 1 teaspoon summer savory, and 3/4 teaspoon freshly ground black pepper. She coats the birds well with this, then bakes them uncovered 1 1/2 hours in a moderate 350° oven.

These are excellent with rice. Betty uses Uncle Ben's Wild and Long Grain Rice mix, preparing it according to the directions on the package. She also sautes a cup of sliced fresh mushrooms and adds these to the rice along with 1 beaten egg. Then she pours the rice mixture into a greased pan, covers it, and pops it into the oven the last 20 minutes the birds are cooking.

ROAST ROCK CORNISH HEN

To make rapturous little roasts of 4 rock cornish game hens, season the inside of the birds with salt, freshly ground black pepper, and a delicate dusting of powdered garlic.

A good stuffing can be prepared by stirring a cup of long-grain white or brown rice in 2 tablespoons of butter or margarine in your frypan over low heat until golden. Then add 1 1/2 cups chicken broth or bouillon, 1/4 cup dry sherry, cover, and allow to bubble until all the liquid is absorbed. Pack loosely in the body cavities and sprinkle everything with paprika. Shape any remaining stuffing into tiny balls to roast along with the birds.

Place the hens, breast sides up, in a shallow roasting pan. Melt a stick of butter or margarine and pour over them. Set in a preheated hot 400° oven, covered with a sheet of foil, for 1/2 hour. Then carefully remove the foil, brush with the drippings, and roast uncovered for 20 minutes or until the drumsticks are soft and pink juice does not ooze out when the thickest part of a thigh is pierced with a sharp fork. Serve at once, perhaps when the sunset is turning the horizon as excitingly crimson as the paprika.

ROCK CORNISH GAME HEN WITH COFFEE

Ever since the momentous day when the coffee berry, according to fable, was discovered on an Abyssinian hillside, more and more people throughout the world have been refreshing themselves with this bracing drink. Here's a way to enjoy the stimulating bean in your meat cookery.

Shake the 4 game hens, one by one, in a paper bag containing 1/2 cup sifted flour seasoned with a teaspoon of salt, a teaspoon of powered instant coffee, and 1/8 teaspoon of freshly ground black pepper. Turning as necessary, brown in 1/4 stick of butter or margarine in a heavy frypan over low heat. Then tip into a well-greased casserole along with a dozen small white onions and an equal number of small scraped carrots.

Bring 2 cups of chicken bouillon to a simmer in a saucepan, stir in 1/4 cup good dry sherry and 1 tablespoon powdered instant coffee, tilt over the fowl, and cover. Bake in a preheated hot 400° oven 1/2 hour. Then add a package of frozen green peas, sprinkle with paprika, recover, and bake another 20 minutes or until the little birds are tender.

While this is going on, prepare enough mixed brown and wild rice for four according to the directions on the package and concoct about 1 1/2 cups of mushroom sauce for your gravy boat.

Start this sauce by melting 3 tablespoons of butter or margarine in a frypan over low heat. Add 1/2 pound of diced mushrooms and saute until shriveled. Then stir in 3 tablespoons sifted flour, first blended into a thin paste with a little water, several drops of the juice from a crushed clove of garlic. Cook 5 minutes over the same conservative heat. Stirring continually, pour in a cup of cream bit by bit. Season with a dissolved beef bouillon cube, a dusting of paprika, and salt to taste. Touch up with a dash of Worcestershire sauce if you like that flavor. This would have been worthy of a toast at any period of history.

Index